Insects
and Spiders
of the World

VOLUME 9
STONE FLY — VELVET WORM

Marshall Cavendish
New York • London • Toronto • Sydney

Marshall Cavendish
99 White Plains Road
Tarrytown, New York 10591

Website: www.marshallcavendish.com

Library of Congress Cataloging-in-Publication Data
Insects and spiders of the world.
    p.   cm.
    Contents: v. 1. Africanized bee–Bee fly — v. 2. Beetle–
Carpet beetle — v. 3. Carrion beetle–Earwig — v. 4. Endangered
species–Gyspy moth v. 5. Harvester ant–Leaf-cutting ant — v. 6.
Locomotion–Orb-web spider — v. 7. Owlet moth–Scorpion —
v. 8. Scorpion fly–Stinkbug — v. 9. Stone fly–Velvet worm —
v. 10. Wandering spider–Zorapteran — v. 11. Index.
    ISBN 0-7614-7334-3 (set) — ISBN 0-7614-7335-1 (v. 1) — ISBN
0-7614-7336-X (v. 2) — ISBN 0-7614-7337-8 (v. 3) — ISBN 0-7614-7338-6
(v. 4) — ISBN 0-7614-7339-4 (v. 5) — ISBN 0-7614-7340-8 (v. 6) — ISBN
0-7614-7341-6 (v. 7) — ISBN 0-7614-7342-4 (v. 8) — ISBN 0-7614-7343-2
(v. 9) — ISBN 0-7614-7344-0 (v. 10) — ISBN 0-7614-7345-9 (v. 11)
    1. Insects. 2. Spiders.   I. Marshall Cavendish Corporation.

QL463 .I732 2003
595.7—dc21

                                                          2001028882

ISBN 0-7614-7334-3 (set)
ISBN 0-7614-7343-2 (volume 9)

Printed in Hong Kong

06 05 04 03 02   6 5 4 3 2 1

Brown Partworks Limited   Marshall Cavendish
Project Editor: Tom Jackson   Editor: Joyce Tavolacci
Subeditor: Jim Martin   Editorial Director: Paul Bernabeo
Managing Editor: Bridget Giles
Design: Graham Curd for WDA
Picture Researcher: Helen Simm
Illustrations: Wildlife Art Limited
Graphics: Darren Awuah, Dax Fullbrook, Mark Walker
Indexer: Kay Ollerenshaw

WRITERS
Dr. Robert S. Anderson   Becca Law
Richard Beatty   Professor Steve Marshall
Dr. Stuart Church   Jamie McDonald
Dr. Douglas C. Currie   Ben Morgan
Trevor Day   Dr. Kieren Pitts
Dr. Arthur V. Evans   Rebecca Saunders
Amanda J. Harman   Dr. Joseph L. Thorley
Dr. Rob Houston   Dr. Gavin Wilson
Anne K. Jamieson

COVER: Leaf-cutting ant **(NHPA)**
TITLE PAGE: Morpho butterfly **(Papilio Photographic)**

PICTURE CREDITS
Agricultural Research Service, USDA: Scott Bauer 545b, 552, 553,
554; **Art Explosion**: 556t; **Artville**: Burke & Triolo 570; **Bruce
Coleman Collection**: Kim Taylor 530r, 542, 563; **Corbis**: Gallo
Images 540, Peter Johnson 532; **Ecoscene**: Grynie Nilz 533;
Educational Images: 537, Ron West 519, 547; **Dr A. V. Evans**:
Image Ideas Inc.: 528; **Steve Marshall**: 517, 558, 571; **Natural
Science Photos**: William Curtis 569, Richard Revels 557; **NHPA**:
Anthony Bannister 545t, 548, 559, 562, James Carmichael Jr. 524,
Daniel Heuchlin 522, 525, Alberto Nardi 516; **Oxford Scientific
Films**: G. I. Bernard 549, Derek Bromhall 573t, J. A. L. Cooke 539,
539, David M. Dennis 527, David Fox 561, Paul Franklin 541, John
Mitchell 538, David Shale 531; **Papilio Photographic**: Robert Pickett
530l; **Hans Pohl**: 565, 566; **Science Photo Library**: Eye of Science 551,
Dr. Morley Read 573b, J. C. Revy 546, David Scharf 520, 523;
Wellcome Trust Photo Library: Audio Visual LSHTM 564

CONTENTS

STONE FLY

Many stone flies live for only a few days, and finding a mate quickly is very important. Males attract females by drumming out mating calls on branches with their abdomens.

Stone flies live in and around freshwater streams or lakes. Adult stone flies range from 0.25 to 2 inches (6 to 51 mm) long. They have long antennae and two pairs of thin, lacy wings. Most of a stone fly's life is spent as a nymph on the gravelly bottom of a stream. Stone fly nymphs blend in well with their stony surroundings since they are dull gray, brown, green, or yellow. The nymphs of a few Southern Hemisphere species, however, live in damp soil.

Folded wings

Most stone flies live in cooler parts of the world, from the snows of the far north to milder parts of the world, such as the United States and Europe. There are around 1,700 species of stone flies, and more than 600 of these live in North America. Stone flies form the order Plecoptera, a word that derives from two Greek words: *pleko*, which means "pleat," and *ptera*, meaning "wings." These refer to the large hind wings that fold like a fan beneath the smaller front pair when the insect is at rest. However, stone flies are not strong fliers, and they rarely travel far from the stream or brook where they hatched. Some stone flies cannot fly at all as they have greatly reduced wings, and a few species have lost them altogether.

Stone flies are an ancient group of insects. Fossil stone flies have been found in 300-million-year-old rocks, and over this huge span of time stone flies have changed little.

▼ *This adult stone fly (right) has just emerged from the skin of the last nymph stage. The old exoskeleton (skin) is to the left.*

Untroubled waters

All animals need oxygen to live. The nymphs of stone flies can survive only in moving waters, like streams and brooks. This is because moving water, especially when it bubbles over rocks and stones, contains a lot of dissolved oxygen. Also, these insects prefer cool regions, because water holds less dissolved oxygen as the temperature rises.

Biologists use stone flies as indicators of the health of highland brooks and streams. A large, healthy population of stone flies in a stream is a good sign that the water is clean and unpolluted. Anglers who are looking to catch fish such as trout watch out for stone flies such as the yellow Sally, because these insects are an important source of food for many freshwater fish.

Life as a nymph

Stone flies do not suddenly change from one body form and lifestyle to another in one dramatic step, in the way a caterpillar changes into a butterfly. Instead, these insects change into adults more gradually. After hatching from their underwater eggs, the nymphs grow successively larger through up to 30 stages, or instars.

They have wing pads, which are saclike growths that contain the developing wings, and two very long filaments on the abdomen, which look like tails. Some stone fly nymphs have gills that stick out from the abdomen like hairy tufts. They use the gills to draw oxygen from the water.

Live fast or grow slow

The nymphs of some stone fly species mature into adults in the same year that they hatch. However, the nymphs of some of the larger species take up to three years to grow from egg to adult. Most stone fly nymphs feed on algae and plant material. Some, however, catch other aquatic insects. They use their long tail filaments to detect movement, or chemicals released by the prey. A few species feed on plants when they are small but switch to animals during later instars.

▲ *Having courted with drumming sounds, these stone flies are mating on a leaf. The male is on top of the larger female. She will drop her eggs onto the water's surface.*

When its development is complete, the nymph swims to the bank, where the adult emerges from the skin of the last nymph instar. This often takes place at night, so the emerging adults avoid predators such as birds.

The exact timing of their emergence is determined by a combination of temperature and day length. In places where a number of different species of stone flies are present, members of each species emerge as adults at different times. This reduces competition between the stone flies for breeding sites, and in feeding species, for food. Sometimes, huge numbers of adults emerge together. However, not all species have a strictly controlled cycle of development. In milder areas, such as along the Pacific coast of North America, adult stone flies can be seen flying all year round.

Brief lives

After all the time spent growing and developing, adult stone flies have short lives. Most males live for just a few days or even hours, while the females may live for a few weeks. Many stone flies do not feed once they are adults and do not even have mouthparts. Their sole role as adults is to breed. Some adult stone flies do feed, usually on algae or lichen. These species tend to live a little longer as adults than the nonfeeding types.

Male stone flies court females by drumming their abdomens on the surfaces on which they are standing. Females detect the vibrations this produces, and those that have yet to breed drum in reply.

The right rhythm

The rhythm of the vibrations that the stone flies produce is species-specific—females of one species do not respond to the drumming of a male from a different species. When a female stone fly drums a reply, the male moves a little closer to the female and drums again. A further

▲ A male and female stone fly court each other by thumping their abdomens on a branch. The insects can detect the vibrations this causes in the wood.

abdomen

KEY FACTS

Name
Yellow Sally stone fly (Isoperla grammatica)

Distinctive features
Fanlike wings that are folded when at rest; golden yellow body

Distribution
Cool freshwater streams throughout the Northern Hemisphere

Behavior
Nymph lives under stones; crawls up plants or rocks before adult emerges

Food
Aquatic insects

Lifespan
Nymph: 1 to 2 years; adult: up to 14 days

Size
Adult is 1 inch (25 mm) long with 2-inch (50-mm) wingspan

◀ *A stone fly nymph crawls through shallow water. The feathery structures along the sides of the body are gills.*

response from the female encourages the male to move yet closer and drum once more. This may happen many times, with the male gradually moving closer and closer to the female. Once the male and female have found each other, they mate. After mating, the female does not respond to the drumming of other males.

Laying eggs in water

Females of some species lay their fertilized eggs loose in the water by dropping them while flying overhead. Other species attach their eggs to rocks in the water with a gluelike gel—this stops them from being washed away by the current. In very cold areas, eggs may be placed in cracks in ice near the edge of the water. A single female stone fly lays as many as 6,000 eggs in her lifetime.

The eggs of most species of stone flies develop for a few weeks in the water, although eggs of larger species may not hatch for several months. The eggs then split down the middle, and the tiny first instar nymphs swim away and begin to feed.

SEE ALSO

- *Alderfly*
- *Caddis fly*
- *Dobsonfly*
- *Dragonfly and damselfly*
- *Lacewing*
- *Mayfly*
- *Sponge fly*

SUCKING LOUSE

Sucking lice are small insects that feed on the blood of a wide range of mammals. They include three human parasites—the head louse, the body louse, and the pubic louse.

Lice belong to the insect order Phthiraptera, which is often divided into the subgroups Anoplura (sucking lice) and Mallophaga (biting lice). There are around 500 species of sucking lice, 70 of which live in North America.

Sucking lice are parasites of mammals. Parasites are organisms that live on or in another host organism. Sucking lice live on the skin of their hosts, mainly rodents and hooved animals, such as cattle. A smaller number of species live on monkeys, apes, and people, and on water-living mammals, such as seals and walruses. A few live on large carnivores such as lions.

Specializing on just one host

Most sucking lice live on just one particular type of mammal, although some can live on more than one closely related species, such as sheep and goats,

▼ *A scanning electron microscope image of a pubic louse. These lice have powerful muscles to lock their claws around hairs. They feed on human blood, leaving bluish marks on the skin.*

for example. An infestation of sucking lice generally causes itching and skin irritation. Occasionally, more serious problems result because some of these lice carry disease-causing organisms.

Shape and size

Sucking lice range in size from a tiny fraction of an inch, right up to about 0.5 inches (1.25 cm) long, depending on the size of their host. These insects have no wings or eyes, and their bodies are flattened from top to bottom, allowing them to move easily through dense hair or fur. Their legs are short and strong, each with a single large claw that varies in shape according to the shape of the host's hairs.

Many species of sucking lice have particular features that suit the lifestyle of their hosts. For example, some lice infest water-living mammals, especially seals and otters. These lice have many flattened, overlapping bristles on their bodies. These bristles trap a bubble of air around the insect's body, allowing the louse to breathe while its host is submerged beneath the waves. Some species may burrow into the thick skin of their host for further protection. Breeding in seal and otter lice coincides with breeding in their hosts, which come on to land to mate and give birth.

Producing the next generation

Sucking lice spend their entire lives on their hosts. The lice mate on the host, although the females can also produce offspring without mating, in a process called parthenogenesis. The eggs are white, oval, and measure around 0.06 inches (1.5 mm) long. They are cemented securely to the shafts of hairs close to the skin of the host animal, using secretions from glands in the female's abdomen.

The developing insect inside the egg has a series of spines on its head—these are used to help the young louse break through the tough eggshell. Hatching takes place after around ten days, and the nymphs must feed on the blood

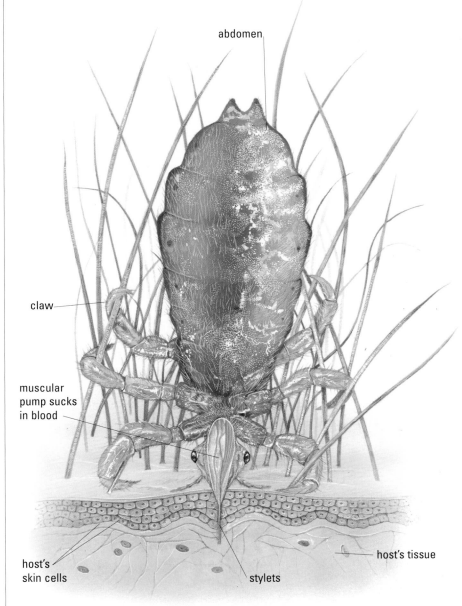

▲ How a sucking louse feeds. The claws hold the louse securely in position as it pierces the skin. Blood from the host is drawn through the stylets, while the salivary glands release chemicals that keep the blood running freely.

of the host within 24 hours or they will die of starvation. The nymphs look like smaller, paler versions of the adult lice. They molt three times during their development. At each stage they become larger, and gradually develop sexual organs, until they are fully adult. This takes just ten days.

Feeding on blood

Sucking lice feed only on the blood of their hosts. Their mouthparts have a sharp, barbed proboscis and three long,

◄ *A tiny head louse clambers through a forest of human hairs.*

needlelike structures called stylets. The louse breaks through its host's skin with its proboscis. Barbs on the stylet help the insect cling on while feeding. Once the proboscis has broken the skin, the louse sticks its stylets into the wound and starts sucking up blood. When it is not feeding, the louse draws the mouth-parts back into its head.

Bacterial partners

While blood is a good food source, it does lack certain nutrients. To overcome this, sucking lice carry tiny bacteria in their gut. The bacteria and lice are partners. The bacteria provide the extra nutrients needed to give the lice a balanced diet, while the lice give the bacteria a safe place to live. Even the eggs contain bacteria, so the nymphs get the right nutrition as soon as they hatch.

Heat and light

Sucking lice move away from light, keeping them near the skin of the host. They are attracted to heat. If the host dies, the lice quickly detect that the body is cooling off and crawl (lice cannot jump) toward the nearest source of heat, which is usually another animal. Scientists think that they can also smell suitable hosts.

Lice and people

There are two main species of sucking lice that attack people. The human louse is divided into two subspecies, the head louse and the body louse. These look very similar, and both measure around 0.1 inches (2.5 mm) long. As their names suggest, head lice live in the hair on the scalp, and body lice live on the body, and also on clothing.

As well as living on people, human lice also infest some species of monkeys. A closely-related species lives on the bodies of apes.

The second species that infests people is the pubic louse, which lives mainly in the pubic hair around the sexual organs but also in beards and under the armpits. It belongs to a family

KEY FACTS

Name
Pubic louse (*Pthirus pubis*)

Distinctive features
Squat, flat body and tiny head, with very stout, clawed legs

Habitat
Human pubic, armpit, and beard hair

Size
Up to 0.1 inches (2.5 mm) long

that includes just one other species, *Pthirus gorillae*, which, as its name suggests, infests similar parts of the bodies of gorillas. Pubic lice cause intense itching and leave a small bluish rash on the skin.

Human lice are transmitted by direct contact or in clothing and bedding. Young schoolchildren often have head lice. Lice are not fussy and will infest any hair, regardless of how clean it is. Head lice are easily passed on by sharing things like combs and hats. The lice glue their eggs to hairs—the eggs are called nits.

Lice that spread disease

Body lice are common where people are crowded together and hygiene is poor, such as during wars or natural disasters. They live mainly in clothing, moving onto the body to feed. Body lice carry a risk that the other human lice do not, because they can pass on serious diseases, such as typhus. During the Russian Revolution, more than three million people may have died from this louse-transmitted disease.

The lice pick up typhus bacteria when they feed on the blood of an infected person. The disease is spread when the lice move to another host. The louse feces contain bacteria, which are rubbed into broken skin when the infested person scratches.

Most sucking lice die after less than a day away from their host, but body lice can survive for up to a week in clothing or bedding, increasing the chances of these lice passing on the bacteria.

KEY FACTS

Name
Head louse
(*Pediculus
humanus capitis*)

**Distinctive
features**
Flattened, with
pale body and
strong claws
on legs for
gripping hairs

Habitat
Lives only on
the human body,
especially on
the scalp

Breeding
Female lays eggs
on hairs close to
the scalp; eggs are
called nits; nymph
hatches after
around ten days
and must begin
feeding quickly

Food
Human blood

Size
Up to 0.1 inches
(2.5 mm) long

◀ *A human head louse clinging to a human hair. The insect has cemented an egg to the hair—the nymph will emerge through the perforated cap at the top.*

SEE ALSO

- *Biting louse*
- *Disease carrier*
- *Pest*

SUN SPIDER

For their body size, sun spiders have the strongest mouthparts of any animal. Armed with these powerful weapons, sun spiders are fierce hunters, using their scissorlike mouthparts to crush their prey into a soggy pulp.

Although they look very similar to true spiders, sun spiders belong to the order of arachnids called Solifugae. These animals are distinguished by their huge chelicerae (mouthparts), which

▼ *A sun spider feasts on a desert cricket using its two massive chelicerae.*

they use to crush prey. Like most other types of arachnids, sun spiders have two body segments, the cephalothorax (fused head and midbody) and the abdomen. The abdomen has ten segments, which are clearly visible in most species. Sun spiders are covered by rows of tiny hairs that help the arachnids sense their surroundings.

Big mouth strikes again

Sun spiders possess the strongest mouthparts, in proportion to their body size, of any animal. A sun spider has two chelicerae, each made up of two toothed segments that work like a pair of scissors. In some species, the chelicerae are rubbed together to produce sounds when the animal is threatened. The chelicerae are attached to the cephalothorax, which contains the powerful muscles required to move the legs and chelicerae.

Two legs over

At first glance, sun spiders appear to possess five pairs of legs rather than four. A closer inspection shows that the first pair are actually pedipalps. The sun spider uses its pedipalps to hold food and other objects. The pedipalps of sun spiders are larger than those of other arachnids and are often used as feelers. They also have sticky pads at the end that allow sun spiders to grab prey and climb up smooth surfaces.

Sun spiders have long, slender legs, allowing the animal to run very quickly. Each leg ends with two claws. Each of the last two pairs of legs also possess

◄ Galeodes *sun spiders are common in the deserts of North Africa. This one is feeding on a young desert mouse, mashing the corpse with its powerful chelicerae.*

five triangular structures known as racquet organs. Scientists think that these organs are used to detect the smell of prey or potential mates.

Mysterious strangers

Despite their size and fearsome appearance, very little is known about the biology or behavior of these amazing arachnids. However, scientists think that there are around 1,000 species of sun spiders. Most are yellow, brown, or black, with bodies ranging from 0.5 to 3 inches (1.3 to 7.6 cm) long.

Some species often seem to be bigger than this due to their hairy bodies and wide legspan, which can reach 6 inches (15 cm). Most species live in hot desert regions, and they are very common in Africa and the Middle East. They also live in southern Europe, India, Southeast Asia, and Central and

KEY FACTS

Name
Galeodes arabs
sun spider (no common name)

Distinctive features
Sandy colored; huge chelicerae; male has whiplike flagella at the tops of the chelicerae

Distribution
Desert areas of North Africa

Breeding
Breeding season coincides with rainfall patterns; up to 200 eggs laid in burrows, hatching after two to ten days; female guards the young until they molt

Food
Insects, spiders, scorpions, mice, lizards, and birds

Life span
Up to 1 year

Size
1.5 to 2 inches (4 to 5 cm) long; legspan: 4.75 inches (12 cm)

DISTRIBUTION

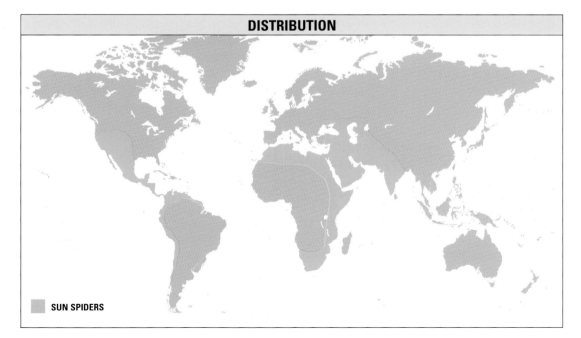

SUN SPIDERS

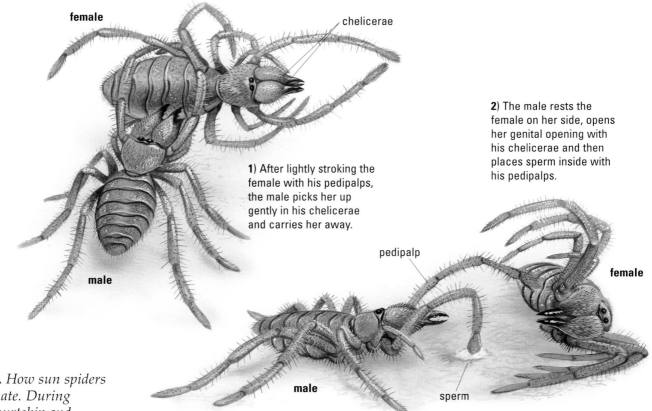

female

chelicerae

2) The male rests the female on her side, opens her genital opening with his chelicerae and then places sperm inside with his pedipalps.

1) After lightly stroking the female with his pedipalps, the male picks her up gently in his chelicerae and carries her away.

pedipalp

female

male

male

sperm

▲ *How sun spiders mate. During courtship and mating, the female keeps still after the male strokes her with his pedipalps. After mating is complete, she takes a little time to recover. Females hunt most in the period between fertilization and egg laying.*

South America. In North America, they live in Florida and the high deserts of the southwestern United States. They can even survive around natural hot springs as far north as Canada.

Most sun spiders live in burrows, which they dig using their first pair of legs. Some species use the same burrow for months, particularly during the breeding season, while others will build a new burrow every night.

Off with her head

Although insect exoskeletons are tough, some parts are stronger than others. The toughest areas are rich in a compound called chitin. When a sun spider catches an insect such as a grasshopper, it first snips off chitin-rich parts of the body, such as the head, wings, and forelegs. The sun spider then quickly mashes and feeds on the softer, more accessible parts of the victim's body, such as the abdomen, thorax (midbody), and hind legs. By focusing on the softer parts of its prey and ignoring tougher, less nutritious areas, the sun spider reduces the time and energy spent during feeding. This is called optimization—the costs are kept as low as possible while the sun spider gains as much energy from the prey item as it can. By optimizing in this way, the sun spider reduces the risk of being caught by a predator while feeding, and more energy is available for finding mates or producing eggs.

Run like the wind
Despite their name, many sun spiders are nocturnal (active at night). Those that are active during the day are extremely quick runners and have often been described as looking like balls of dust being blown across the ground. This resemblance gives the sun spiders their other common name, wind scorpions. To support this active lifestyle, sun spiders have a breathing system that uses tubes to take air into the body. This system is similar to the one used by insects, although it evolved separately.

Eat, drink, and mate
Sun spiders have huge appetites and mouthparts to match. They are all meat eaters, feeding on insects, spiders, scorpions, mice, and lizards. Sun spiders attack animals of a similar size or smaller, and the females are especially aggressive hunters just before laying their eggs. Sun spiders will gorge themselves on prey until they are almost unable to move.

After capturing an insect or small lizard, a sun spider uses its pedipalps to drag the animal toward its huge chelicerae. These then cut up and slice the prey into a soft pulp, which the sun spider sucks up. Sun spiders can be highly specialized in their diets. A species from California crawls into beehives to feed on bees, while another from Colorado eats bedbugs. Others dig burrows into termites' nests to eat the insects inside.

Many people mistakenly believe that sun spiders are venomous. Almost all sun spiders rely solely on the power of their chelicerae to kill other animals. Just one species of sun spider, from southern India, has venom glands. Although next to nothing is known of the biology of this species, it seems to use its venom in a very different way from true spiders. The ends of the chelicerae do not have openings and so they cannot pump venom into victims like a true spider's fangs can. Instead, secretions from the venom glands run down grooves along the outsides of the chelicerae. This venom helps subdue particularly large or aggressive prey.

The chelicerae have other important roles besides prey capture. Although they derive most of the water they need from their food, sun spiders will sometimes use their chelicerae to collect water droplets, which they then drink. Whiplike organs called flagella are attached to the upper parts of the chelicerae of male sun spiders. These may be used to display to other males or to the females prior to courtship.

Swooning sun spiders

Male sun spiders are often smaller than the females, although they generally have longer legs. When a male finds a female, he approaches her cautiously and strokes her body with his pedipalps. This stroking action causes the female to stop moving and to enter a trancelike state, allowing the male to continue his courtship without the risk of being eaten by the female.

After the female is relaxed, the male picks her up using his chelicerae and carries her some distance before placing her on her side on the ground. Using his chelicerae, the male opens the genital opening of the female. He then releases a blob of sperm from his abdomen and transfers it to the female with his chelicerae or pedipalps, depending on the species. The male then retreats to safety before the female rouses.

After care

The female digs a burrow in which she lays around 200 eggs. The eggs of some species hatch within one to three days, while those of others can develop for three or four weeks before hatching takes place. Newly hatched sun spiders are termed post-embryos. They are unable to move and look only a little like adult sun spiders. The females of some species guard their post-embryos from predators during this early stage.

After a week or two, the post-embryos molt into nymphs, which look much more like the fully grown adults. The nymphs soon leave their mothers to live alone. Adult sun spiders live for about one year in the wild.

SEE ALSO

- *Arthropod*
- *False scorpion*
- *Feeding*
- *Scorpion*
- *Spider*
- *Tick and mite*
- *Whip scorpion*

▼ *A sun spider holds its pedipalps out in front, using them as feelers in the same way many insects use their antennae.*

SWALLOWTAIL

Swallowtails are named for their hind wings, which often have tail-like extensions similar to the tail streamers of swallows.

There are around 600 species in the swallowtail butterfly family, which includes some of the largest and most brilliantly colored of all butterflies, such as the African giant swallowtail. This butterfly is black with bold yellow stripes, and has a 10-inch (25-cm) wingspan. Smaller swallowtails include the dragontails, which have wingspans of less than 2 inches (5 cm). Apollo butterflies and bird-wings are also part of the swallowtail family.

Wonderful wings

Swallowtails are best recognized by their wings. Both pairs are large, and each hind wing generally has a tail-like streamer at the base. The size and shape of these streamers varies. The old world swallowtail has small, plain black tails, while the North American giant swallowtail has larger tails that each have a yellow spot. Tails can also differ within the same species. For example, mocker swallowtails live throughout

▼ *A tiger swallow-tail feeds on nectar. Like many other types of swallow-tails, this species is brightly colored.*

Africa. Males have tail streamers, but throughout most of their range, females do not. However, in Madagascar and the Ethiopian Highlands, populations of mocker butterflies have evolved in isolation for millions of years. In these regions, the females retain their tails. Other members of the swallowtail family, such as dragontail and clubtail butterflies, have larger tails. The tails of green dragontail butterflies are longer than the rest of their wings put together. Hovering is rare in butterflies, but dragontails can hover above flowers as they feed on the nectar within.

◄ *Old world swallowtail caterpillars stop feeding and use their osmeteria to release unpleasant chemicals when they are threatened by a parasitic wasp.*

feeding caterpillars

osmeterium

parasitic wasp

Many species have two or more different color patterns. These are called morphs. For example, there are two morphs of eastern tiger swallowtails—a shiny blue–black morph and a yellow and black one.

Beautiful bird-wings
Bird-wings are among the most beautiful of all butterflies, with blue, green, and yellow scales that give their wings and bodies a metallic shine. Bird-wing butterflies generally live in warm, tropical parts of Australia and Southeast Asia. Due to their coloring and large size, bird-wings have been collected a great deal by enthusiasts. As a result, many species are now very rare. The greatest threat to these butterflies,

however, is habitat loss. As people cut down tropical rain forests for agriculture or construction, the habitat gradually becomes fragmented. Small patches of forest cannot sustain butterfly populations, which disappear.

Show and smell
Swallowtail caterpillars and pupae use a range of tactics to deter predators and parasites. A caterpillar has an organ called an osmeterium behind its head. This forked structure is usually held inside the body. When threatened, the caterpillar pushes its osmeterium out, using the pressure of the hemolymph (blood) inside the body cavity. The osmeterium releases strong-smelling chemicals that drive enemies away. As

KEY FACTS

Name
Old world swallowtail (*Papilio machaon*)

Distinctive features
Large black and yellow wings with tail streamers; red eyespots at the base of each hind wing

Habitat
From grasslands to marshes and mountains

Breeding
Female lays eggs on food plants

Food
Caterpillar feeds on milk parsley

Size
Wingspan: 2.5 to 4 inches (6.5 to 10 cm)

adult swallowtail

well as producing an unpleasant smell, some caterpillars have eyespots on their heads that can startle predators

Good copies

The young of swallowtails are master mimics. The pupa of the Rajah Brookes bird-wing, from Southeast Asia, resembles a dead, dried leaf hanging from a plant, while the caterpillars of checkered swallowtails look just like bird droppings. A number of swallowtail caterpillars feed on poisonous types of plants, and use the toxins for their own protection. Many species, however, do not have defensive

chrysalis

cremaster

▲ *An adult old world swallowtail allows its wings to harden, having just emerged from its chrysalis. This is attached to a twig by the cremaster.*

▲ *A caterpillar hatches from its egg.*

chemicals. These butterflies often mimic other, poisonous species. For example, various morphs of female false-monarch swallowtails mimic a variety of different species of poisonous monarch butterflies. Males, however, are not mimics; they look like other swallowtails and are readily eaten by birds.

Life from egg to adult

The rounded eggs of swallowtails are laid on or near plants that are eaten by the caterpillars. Many tropical bird-wings feed on pipevines. Young anise swallowtail caterpillars feed on parsley leaves, switching to the flowers when they grow larger. Some swallowtails feed on crops but only occasionally become pests. The caterpillars tend not to be hairy, but many have defensive spikes on their bodies. Some have bright and striking colors that warn predators of their poisonous nature.

To pupate, swallowtail caterpillars attach themselves to plants in an upright position, held by a silk girdle and a structure called a cremaster. The cremaster is a series of small hooks that grip a silk pad that the insect sticks to the plant. Having completed their development, the adults emerge, dry their wings, and fly off to find food and mates, often releasing chemicals into the air to attract a partner.

SEE ALSO

• *Endangered species*
• *Monarch butterfly*
• *Moth and butterfly*

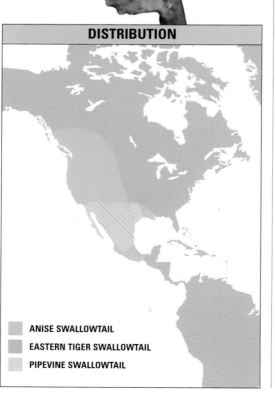

DISTRIBUTION

ANISE SWALLOWTAIL

EASTERN TIGER SWALLOWTAIL

PIPEVINE SWALLOWTAIL

SWARMING

Large groups of insects are called swarms. Swarms of locusts can contain many millions of insects and eat vast quantities of crops. Other insect swarms are much smaller and contain a few hundred insects looking for mates.

Insects swarm for many different reasons. They may need to migrate from one place to another, for instance, or they might meet in a certain place so they can choose mates. Insect groups can become spectacularly large, none more so than the swarms occasionally formed by locusts.

Locusts are well-known for their swarms, but they usually live alone. However, when conditions become crowded, the nymphs begin to develop into a different, migratory form of locust. These locusts group together to form vast swarms, or plagues. Locust plagues can contain many millions of insects. They can devastate hundreds of square miles of crops in just a few days. Scientists are working hard to understand the causes of locust swarming behavior and how to prevent it.

Reasons to swarm

Social insects often migrate in swarms. Swarms of bees form to find new nest sites. Other insects, including mayflies, caddis flies, crane flies, mosquitoes, and midges, swarm to find mates. These insects may join a swarm every day of their short adult lives. Most insects that form mating swarms develop as underwater larvae. After becoming flying

▲ *A swarm of migratory locusts from northwest Africa. These insects have plagued people for thousands of years. The swarms often arrive at nightfall and consume huge amounts of plant material.*

adults, these insects do little but attempt to find mates and lay eggs. The adults take to the air and form swarms on river banks and lakesides on summer evenings. Swarms of midges and mosquitoes often form over objects such as tree stumps or gate posts. These objects act as landmarks, helping the insects find the swarming point.

The insects then move in a dancing flight, ducking in and out of the swarm. Some mayflies perform up-and-down dancing movements, while others fly from side to side.

Mainly males

In most species, only the males join mating swarms. The purpose of swarming seems to be to attract females. Females briefly fly into swarms and pair up with males. Pairs of insects leave the swarm to mate. Swarming may have other functions. If males must display to attract females, it pays to display together. That way, each individual male runs a smaller risk of being caught and eaten by a predator. Even though swarms are easy for predators to spot, the individuals in the middle of the swarm are safe from predators such as bats, which usually pick off individuals from the edges of swarms. Displaying together also makes a larger signal that is visible to many more females over much greater distances.

The rules of competition

Mating swarms are also part of a sophisticated behavioral system that allows insects to choose the best mates. The females force the males to swarm by refusing to mate with any males that do not. In swarms, the males are often

▲ *A cloud of male nonbiting midges. These insects compete for females. Those near the center of the swarm stand a lower risk of being caught by a flying predator, such as a bat.*

SEE ALSO

- Crane fly
- Gnat
- Grasshopper and cricket
- Midge
- Mosquito

forced to compete. Male lovebugs, for instance, jostle each other while swarming and compete to occupy the bottom positions in the swarm. Each female enters the swarm from the bottom and pairs off with the first male she encounters, which is usually a large, fit male that has won the battle to occupy the bottom position. The largest male caddis flies and mayflies in swarms also tend to get the most females. In the case of midges, however, it is usually the smallest, most symmetrical males that gain the females, because they are most agile and are better at catching females that enter the swarm.

Mass gatherings

Mating swarms can be just as spectacular, large, and dense as migratory swarms. The numbers of individual insects can be vast. In Lake Erie, in North America, some types of mayflies emerge all at once and swarm together as well. The huge mayfly swarms can lead to so-called brown-outs—blizzards of insects. The midge swarms around Lake Victoria in Africa are similarly vast. The swarms are sometimes so dense that people have choked to death.

A reversal of roles

Dance flies are large predatory flies, one of many predators attracted to swarms of midges. Male dance flies capture midges from the swarms and take them as mating gifts for females. Unusually, it is the female dance flies that swarm, in a very rare case of sexual role reversal. The females in the swarm compete with each other to receive the males and their gifts of dead midges.

SYMBIOSIS

Symbiosis describes relationships between different species of organisms. The insect world is rich in symbiotic relationships between insect species, and with mites, plants, and fungi.

In any given habitat, different species of animals and plants do not live in isolation from each other. Instead, they are constantly interacting, for example, as predators and their prey, or two plant eaters competing for food. Some species have particularly close relationships—biologists call this symbiosis.

There are three main types of symbiotic relationships. Relationships in which both partners (or symbionts) benefit are called mutualisms. The benefits vary from food and shelter to protection from predators. Sometimes, one partner benefits while the other remains unaffected. This is called commensalism. Commensal relationships often involve a large animal transporting a smaller one.

The third main type of symbiosis is called parasitism. Parasitism is an unequal relationship between two symbionts—one, the parasite, benefits at the expense of the other, the host. Some parasites kill their hosts—these are called parasitoids. Others, known as kleptoparasites, steal food but do not actually feed on the host.

Plants and insects

Many symbiotic relationships involve plants and insects. Insect pollination is a mutualism. Insects provide plants with the opportunity to deliver small amounts of pollen direct to other flowers of the same species, while the insect receives food in the form of pollen or nectar in return. Many plants and

KEY WORDS

Commensalism
A relationship in which one partner benefits and the other is neither harmed nor helped

Mutualism
A relationship in which both partners benefit

Parasitism
Unequal partnership where one organism benefits at the other partner's expense

Symbiont
One of the partners in a symbiotic relationship

Symbiosis
A relationship between two different species

◀ A hover fly feeds on flower pollen. The pollen from this flower may be transferred to the next flower the fly feeds on, fertilizing that flower's eggs and producing seeds.

insects have evolved together over millions of years, and are unable to survive without each other. For example, fig trees cannot produce seeds without pollination by fig wasps, and fig wasps cannot breed outside a fig fruit.

Another close relationship exists between some acacia trees and acacia ants. The plants have large, hollow thorns that provide a sheltered nest-space for the ants. Colonies containing as many as 30,000 ants live among the thorns of a single acacia tree.

Not only does the tree provide a home, it offers food as well. The acacia produces nectar for the ants, as well as protein-rich nodules at the tips of the leaves. The ants remove these structures and carry them back to the nest. In return for this massive investment, the ants protect the tree against plant-eating insects that attempt to browse on the leaves and flowers. The ants' stings are so painful that even animals such as goats are driven off. The ants also remove fungal spores around the tree that would otherwise cause diseases. They keep the ground around the trunk free of other plants, such as parasitic vines. Removing these plants reduces competition for soil nutrients and water.

In providing for their ants, acacias use resources that other plants reserve for producing defensive chemicals. If the ants are removed, the acacias die in less than a year, because they have no other way of defending themselves. Similarly, the ants cannot survive without the food and shelter provided by the acacias.

Insects and microorganisms

Many insects contain colonies of tiny single-celled microorganisms, such as bacteria, inside their bodies. They help digest the food, and may provide extra nutrients for the insects. Many fleas contain microorganisms that help them digest blood. Wood is particularly difficult to digest. Termites and some beetles have microorganisms in their guts that break down wood, releasing sugars. These tiny organisms are also important for wood roaches. When they molt, the nymphs lose their internal microorganism colony, so they eat feces of other roaches to gain a new one.

Symbiotic microorganisms sometimes live outside the body. Leaf-cutting ants and some termites have close relationships with fungi. The insects provide the fungi with food and a place to live. In return, the insects eat some of the fungal fruiting bodies. The fungi break down plant material that the ants would otherwise be unable to digest. Ambrosia beetles introduce fungi to their tunnels in wood. Their larvae eat the fungi, while the fungi breaks down the wood of the tree, sometimes killing it.

▼ *A colony of ants living inside the thorns of a bullhorn acacia tree. The ants feed on the plant's nectar and nutritious leaf nodules. In return, they protect the plant from herbivores, and remove other plants that might compete with it.*

worker ant

leaf nodule

acacia thorn

ant larva

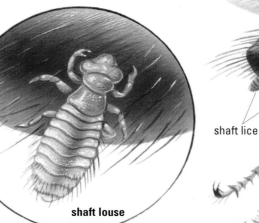

louse fly

shaft lice

shaft louse

◀ *A blood-sucking louse fly searches for a bird to feed on. Clinging to the fly's abdomen are shaft lice which feed on bird feathers. When the fly lands on a bird, the lice jump off.*

Commensal relationships

Some aquatic chironomid midge larvae attach themselves to larger aquatic insects, such as dragonfly nymphs. The nymphs keep predators away from the larvae, but do not benefit—this is an example of a commensal relationship.

A common commensal relationship is known as phoresy. This is where one symbiont hitches a ride on the other. For example, many biting lice are parasites of birds. The little insects usually move from one host to another when birds come into contact with each other in roosts or nests. However, sometimes the lice switch to a new roost by clinging to the bodies of blood-sucking flies, which also feed on birds.

This is risky, because most lice feed on just one species of bird, while the flies are less picky. There is no guarantee that the lice will find themselves on the right kind of bird. Phoresy is used by lice only when conditions become very crowded.

Master hitchhikers

Many species of mites regularly use larger animals to get from place to place. For example, some mites wait on flowers for bees or ants before hitching a ride back to the insect's nest, where they feed on debris and dead insects.

Japanese spruce beetles tunnel into damaged trees, often killing them. Some species of mites clamber aboard the beetles and are transported from tree to tree in this way. They feed on debris and other mites inside the tunnel. One species of fungi is carried by the mites—the fungi grow in the tunnels, perhaps providing food for the young of the beetle.

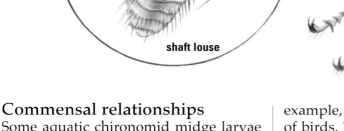

DISTRIBUTION

ACACIA ANT

▲ *A moth caterpillar feeds on a leaf, while a parasitic fly larva feeds on the caterpillar. The fly is a parasitoid — it will eventually kill the caterpillar.*

Sometimes, phoresy is used to attack another animal. Human botflies attach their eggs to a mosquito. When the mosquito lands on a cow or a person, the eggs hatch and the larvae burrow into the skin of the host.

Sharing a home

Sometimes, a commensal relationship involves a symbiont benefiting from sharing the home of another. For example, many different types of beetles live inside ants' nests, while some solitary bees make their nests in the sides of termites' mounds. Meadow ants specialize in making their nests in old mole hills.

▶ *A giant carpenter bee queen, with a close-up of her mite pouch.*

SEE ALSO

- Cockroach
- Defense
- Feeding
- Insect evolution
- Pollination
- Warble fly and botfly

The weird world of parasites

Many insects and arachnids are parasites of other animals. Some, such as sucking lice, bed bugs, and fleas, pierce the skin to drink body fluids, as do ticks. Biting lice feed on hair and feathers. Some parasites, like botfly larvae, actually live inside their hosts. Many insects kill their hosts after growing and developing inside—these are called parasitoids. Many wasps and flies are parasitoids. Most attack other insects and spiders, although some lay their eggs inside other animals, such as earthworms.

Some animals are kleptoparasites—they steal food from others. Spiderwebs form a rich source of food for many kleptoparasites. Tiny dewdrop spiders steal from larger orb-web spiders, and male scorpion flies take dead insects from webs to present as gifts to females. Sometimes, kleptoparasites live on the animals they steal from. Robber flies often have tiny kleptoparasitic flies living on their bodies. The kleptoparasites steal some of the liquid that seeps from puncture wounds in the bodies of the robber flies' prey.

Bees and mites

Although many mites are parasites of bees, some species live in harmony with these insects. For example, the females of some species of carpenter bees have pouches in their abdomens that hold symbiotic mites. The mites lay their eggs on bee pupae. The young mites feed on discarded pupal skins and help stop fungi from infecting the developing insects. When a new queen sets off to build a new nest, she gathers some mites, storing them in the pouch and releasing them when a new nest is established.

symbiotic mites in pouch

giant carpenter bee queen

TARANTULA

Among the largest of all spiders, most tarantulas live in silk-lined burrows in the ground, ambushing insects and small vertebrates. Some females can live for 20 years or more.

Although tarantulas pose very little risk to humans, many people still think they are very dangerous. Of the 800 or so species of tarantulas, most live in the tropical Americas, but some, such as baboon spiders, live in Africa, and there are species in Asia and Australia. In the United States, tarantulas live in southern and southwestern states, as far east as the Mississippi River.

Tarantula colors range from soft tan, through reddish brown, to dark brown or black, depending on the species. The United States is home to mostly smaller species of tarantulas, up to around 2 inches (5 cm) long. However, the world's largest spider is a tarantula. The body of the goliath tarantula from tropical South America grows up to 5 inches (12.5 cm) long, and its legspan can reach 1 foot (30.5 cm) across.

Inside the tarantula body

On the underside of a tarantula's abdomen are four slits through which the spider draws in air. These lead to breathing organs, called book lungs. These are named for the membranes through which oxygen moves into the hemolymph (blood); they are stacked

▼ *A Mexican red-kneed tarantula. These large spiders grow up to 5.5 inches (14 cm) across. They are popular pets but are now rare in the wild.*

side by side like the pages of a book. The hemolymph is pumped into the body cavity of the spider, reaching the parts of the body, such as the muscles, where the oxygen is required.

A tarantula's brain is located in its cephalothorax (fused head and mid-body). It consists of two clusters of nerves and acts as a control center for the spider's body. Nerves branch off to every part of the body. Even the spider's hairs are connected to the nervous system. Tarantulas have eight eyes—three on each side of the cephalothorax with a pair in between, and most species have large, conspicuous fangs attached to their chelicerae (mouthparts).

Tarantulas have thick tufts of hairs between a pair of claws at the ends of each leg. The tip of each hair is divided into thousands of tiny filaments, each with a thin coating of liquid. This allows the spider to grip smooth surfaces. As the spider walks, the pressure of the fluid inside its body cavity spreads the tufts out, increasing the area of filaments in contact with

the ground. The sticky filaments may also help the tarantula hold on to struggling prey. Like other spiders, tarantulas also use fluid pressure to extend their legs when walking.

DISTRIBUTION

GOLIATH TARANTULA

MEXICAN RED-KNEED TARANTULA

KEY FACTS

Name
Mexican red-kneed tarantula (*Brachypelma smithii*)

Distinctive features
Dark brown with orange bands on legs

Breeding
Females lay 700 eggs each year

Size
Legspan is up to 5.5 inches (14 cm) across

▼ *Some tarantulas are called bird-eating spiders. This goliath tarantula is eating a nestling.*

▶ *A pair of Aphonopelma tarantulas mating. Males wait their turn to mate without competing, and the female shows little aggression toward the male during courtship and mating.*

Excavating a home

The females of some species dig deep burrows into dry soil and line them with silk. The Texas brown tarantula uses silk to excavate and transport soil during burrow construction. Soil sticks to the silk, and the spider gathers up the threads into a bundle. The spider carries the bundles in its chelicerae and deposits them at the surface. Other tarantulas do not dig burrows. They rest during the day in holes in tree trunks, gaps between stones, or in abandoned rodent holes.

Tarantulas spend most of the day hidden away, becoming active in the early evening and throughout the night when they hunt for food. This slow lifestyle allows them to go for a very long time between meals.

Catching a meal

Tarantulas do not spin webs. Instead, they rely on strength and speed to catch unsuspecting prey. Lines of silk trail from their burrows, acting as tripwires that alert the waiting tarantula to the presence of prey close by. Some tarantulas live in trees and attack by jumping onto their victims.

When prey is nearby, the tarantula ambushes the animal and delivers a venomous bite with its large fangs, paralyzing the victim. Some of the larger species feed on animals such as frogs, lizards, small snakes, and even small birds. However, most prey on

How tarantulas got their name

Around the town of Taranto in southern Italy in the mid-thirteenth century, many peasants were stricken with a strange disease during harvest time. It caused a bout of depression followed by involuntary spasms that made the victim appear to be dancing. People thought that this was caused by the bite of a spider, which came to be known as a tarantula, after the town.

However, scientists have shown that the venom of this spider has no effect on people. The disease, called tarantism, may have been caused by a neurological (nervous) illness similar to St. Vitus dance. Some of the epidemics that were reported by scholars of the time may have been induced by mass hysteria. The tarantella, a frenzied Italian folk dance, is based on the movements of victims of this illness.

The original tarantula is actually a type of wolf spider. Today, the name has passed to a completely different group of spiders, which are sometimes also called bird-eating spiders.

Hairy defenses

Many tarantulas use irritating, or urticating, hairs to protect themselves against predators. Located on the abdomen, these hairs are covered by hundreds of tiny hooks that cause severe itching when in contact with skin, especially around the nose and eyes. The hairs narrow toward the base so they are easily detatched. A few tree-living tarantula species rely on bringing the urticating-hair region into direct contact with the skin of the predator. Most, however, vibrate their back legs rapidly against their abdomens, releasing a cloud of hairs. Urticating hairs are mainly used as a defense against vertebrates (animals with backbones) such as coatis and monkeys.

Only New World tarantulas have urticating hairs. With such an effective defense mechanism, these spiders do not need to produce powerful venom. By contrast, African and Asian species lack urticating hairs, and their venom is much more potent. These tarantulas are also more aggressive, and they are quick to attack any threat.

insects, such as crickets, beetles, and grasshoppers. After paralyzing their prey, tarantulas inject enzymes into the prey's body. The enzymes break down the internal organs into a soup, and the spiders suck up this liquid meal.

Staying alive

Being formidable predators themselves, tarantulas do not have many natural enemies, although snakes, birds, and mammals such as coatis will sometimes feed on them. Many tarantulas have irritating hairs on their abdomens to protect themselves. Goliath tarantulas use a different series of hairs to ward off predators. Some hairs on the femora (the longest sections) of the front two pairs of legs and on the pedipalps (leglike appendages on the cephalo-thorax) have hooks, while others bear a plume of short filaments. When the spider is threatened, it alternately attaches and pulls apart the hooks and the filaments to produce a loud hissing sound. This sound warns vertebrate predators that the spider is well armed with both irritating hairs and venom.

Smaller species and younger individuals are sometimes attacked by mantises, scorpions, and other spiders. The main enemies of tarantulas, however, are spider-hunting wasps, which paralyze the spiders and lay an egg inside. When the egg hatches, the larva feeds on the still-living spider before maturing into an adult wasp. The larvae of some flies live as parasites on the bodies of tarantulas, moving down to feast on the mixture of saliva and digested organs of prey as the spider feeds.

Continuing the line

In the fall, a male tarantula spins a web, around two-thirds the size of its body. It deposits droplets of sperm onto the web. The male then draws the sperm into a bulb at the tip of its pedipalps before going in search of a female. The male locates the female by detecting chemicals called phero-mones that are in the silk of the female's burrow. The male performs a courtship dance, subduing the female by stroking her with his legs. Using his pedipalps, he places the sperm into her repro-ductive opening before retreating.

When two male *Aphonopelma* tarantulas meet close to the burrow of a female, there is no aggression or competition for mating rights. Both males mate in quick succession; neither guards the female

▼ *This African baboon spider is displaying its fangs to warn off an enemy. Baboon spiders possess potent venom and are quick to attack when threatened.*

◄ *Spiderlings emerge from the burrow of a female Colombian lesser black tarantula. The young stay within the safety of the burrow for several weeks before leaving.*

KEY FACTS

Name
Goliath tarantula
(*Theraphosa blondi*)

Distinctive features
Chocolate brown;
with body length of
around 5 inches
(12.5 cm) and
legspan up to
1 foot (30.5 cm),
the largest spider
in the world

Behavior
When threatened
makes hissing
sound; can
also release
urticating hairs

Food
Large insects,
lizards, birds, and
small mammals

Life span
Female lives up
to 20 years

after mating. This is unusual; generally, the last male to mate with a female fertilizes most of the eggs. Female *Aphonopelma* spiders are passive and do not attack their suitors.

After mating, the female tarantula stores the sperm in her body. She modifies part of her burrow into a sac, into which up to 1,000 eggs are laid. The female then seals off the sac. She stands guard over the sac until the eggs hatch.

Six to nine weeks after being deposited into the cocoon, the young spiderlings break free. Two or three weeks later, they move away from the burrow.

Long lives
Tarantulas may develop for a long time before they are ready to breed, up to ten years in some species. Forced to wander far and wide in search of females, male tarantulas live risky lives and seldom live for longer than a couple of years after reaching adulthood. Females,

however, are among the longest-lived of all invertebrates (animals without backbones) and can live for 20 years or more in the wild. *Eurypelma californicum* is common throughout the southwestern United States; a captive individual of this species lived for almost 30 years, shedding its old skin each year.

Tarantulas and people
Despite their reputation, tarantulas do not usually bite people unless they are provoked. In most cases, bites simply cause some swelling and irritation and are a little like beestings. However, the bites of some species, especially the African and Asian tarantulas, can be very painful.

Because of their dramatic appearance, long life spans, and generally peaceful nature, many people keep tarantulas as pets. However, over-collecting for the pet trade has severely affected populations of a number of species, including the familiar Mexican red-kneed tarantula.

SEE ALSO
- *Funnel-web spider*
- *Spider*
- *Trap-door spider*

TERMITE

Although termites are often confused with ants, because they also live in complex societies, their closest relatives are cockroaches and mantises. Termites build some of the biggest nests of any animal.

Termites are among the most numerous insects in some tropical forests—there may be up to 1,300 termites in each square foot (14,000 per sq m) of forest floor. More than 2,500 species live around the world, with 44 species present in North America.

A wood diet
Termites are divided into two groups, lower and higher termites. Lower termites live in and feed on wood. The fibers that give wood its structure are very difficult to digest. Lower termites have symbiotic bacteria and protozoa (single-celled organisms) in their guts that break down wood, releasing nutrients. The adults feed the microorganisms to each new generation to ensure that the young can digest their food.

Higher termites have bacteria but no protozoa in their guts. Some higher termites deal with the problems of digesting wood in a different way. Wood passes through the guts of these insects undigested. In the nest, the termites use their wood-filled droppings to build combs, on which they then grow fungus. The fungus breaks down the wood pulp, and the termites feed on the fungus.

The caste system
Like other social insects, there are several different types of termites, called castes, in a colony. The most common termite caste is the worker. Workers are adaptable and are able to carry out the many tasks required to maintain the nest and care for the brood (eggs and

young termites). Worker termites are typically pale and soft-bodied, for which they are sometimes called white ants. These insects are not very tough and are easily picked off by predators, so they tend to look for food in the safety of tunnels in soil or wood, rather than above ground.

Child labor
In contrast to other social insects, such as honeybees and ants, termite workers can be either male or female. Termites undergo incomplete metamorphosis, in which the nymphs (young) gradually develop into adults. Unlike the young of

▲ *Orange termite soldiers stand guard as the smaller white workers repair damage to a tunnel.*

other social insects, which remain helpless until they pupate, termite nymphs are active and help with the work of the colony.

Soldier termites, defenders of the nest, are larger and more powerful than the workers. Each has a large, heavily armored head. In many species, the soldiers have huge, pincerlike mouthparts. In others, the soldiers' mouthparts are like those of the workers, but their snouts are extended to form nozzles, through which they shoot a sticky liquid that dries in the air. This gums up the legs and mouths of attackers, generally ants or other termites.

Exploding termites

Soldiers of one species of termite, *Globitermes sulphureus*, have a very unusual defense. They have enormous glands that produce a sticky glue—these extend through the thorax (mid-

The good and the bad

Termites are important for the health of their habitats. By breaking down wood and other plant material that most other animals cannot eat, termites help recycle energy and nutrients. In the grasslands of west Africa, for example, termites eat more than a quarter of all the dead plants. Before people introduced cattle and sheep to Australia, termites were, and in some places remain, the main plant eaters.

However, termites can also cause serious problems. Some, such as the eastern subterranean termite, build their nests in wooden parts of buildings. They eat their way through houses and other buildings, causing billions of dollars worth of damage each year.

body) and into the abdomen. However, the glands do not have openings to the outside. Instead, when the soldier grapples with an enemy such as an ant, its abdominal wall spasms and violently splits open the gland. The termite dies, but its explosive suicide is not in vain. The glue from the gland traps the ant, which is then killed by other termites alerted by chemicals released by the soldier in its death throes.

termite soldiers

driver ants

▲ *A squad of termite soldiers repel attacking army ants by spraying them with a sticky liquid. The chemicals in the liquid are mixed as they shoot out of the termites' heads to avoid blocking the nozzle.*

DISTRIBUTION

EASTERN SUBTERRANEAN TERMITE

KEY FACTS

Name
Eastern sub-terranean termite (*Reticulitermes flavipes*)

Distinctive features
Huge colonies that cover 0.5 acres (0.2 hectares)

Behavior
Most destructive pest in the United States, feeding on timber in buildings

Size
Worker and male: 0.2 inches (5 mm) long; soldier: 0.25 inches (7 mm) long; queen: up to 3.5 inches (9 cm) long

Reproduction

Termite colonies are based around a pair of adults, called the king and queen. Once a colony has become established, it produces a generation of winged, fertile individuals, which swarm from the nest. When they land, they pair up, lose their wings, and dig a small nest chamber. Unlike male ants and bees, which die soon after mating, king termites live alongside their queens, mating with them at regular intervals. Together, they raise the first generation of worker termites, feeding them chewed plant material.

All ant workers are female, but termite workers can be of either sex. The first group of workers takes over nest building and care of the young, leaving their parents free to produce more and more offspring. A mature queen can lay up to 2,000 eggs each day. She becomes so swollen with eggs that she may reach up to ten times her previous size, and must be cared for by the workers.

For the first few generations, all the offspring of the king and queen are workers, dedicated to expanding the nest. Eventually, some nymphs grow into soldiers, and, after several years, the king and queen produce winged termites, which continue the cycle.

Master architects

Termites are skillful builders. Many higher termites build their nests from soil particles, saliva, and their own droppings. In warm regions, termite nests can be spectacular mounds up to 30 feet (9 m) high, with extremely tough outer walls to keep out enemies that would otherwise feast on the termites inside. Termites face two major problems when they build their mounds: controlling the temperature and and keeping a flow of fresh air through the nest.

▼ *Inside the mound of a higher temite. The king and queen live in the royal chamber. The workers tend to the fungus, which grows on the comb. This comb is made from the termites' own wood-filled droppings.*

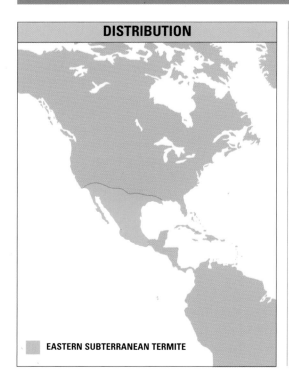

cooling tunnel

central chimney

wood-filled droppings

fungus comb

royal chamber

◀ *A worker termite removes an egg from the hugely swollen abdomen of the colony's queen.*

SEE ALSO

- *Ant*
- *Defense*
- *Metamorphosis*
- *Praying mantis*
- *Social insect*
- *Symbiosis*

A mound may hold millions of termites and large fungus gardens. Temperatures can soar, and with so many insects inside, the amount of oxygen within the nest can drop to low levels.

Some termites control the temperature inside the nest by modifying the shape of the mound. One Australian species builds a mound that is flattened to face the east and west. The north and south sides, which face the midday Sun, are very thin. The wider sides face the weaker early morning and late afternoon Sun. In this way, the colony maintains the correct temperature.

Some higher termites have more complicated cooling systems. Their massive mounds have chimneys that come up from the center of the nest. Warm air rises up the chimney and into a network of narrow passages near the surface of the mound. The air cools and draws in oxygen. The cooler air sinks back into the nest, passing over a series of vanes. The workers keep these vanes

moist, which cools the air further. The termites' cooling system is so efficient that engineers are starting to use its principles in building design. The Eastgate building in Harare, Zimbabwe, is built like a giant termite mound; it does not need any air conditioning, which saves a great deal of energy.

▼ *A soldier subterranean termite. These insects use their powerful mandibles to defend the nest against enemies, such as ants.*

THRIPS

Although they are rarely seen, thrips are important plant pollinators, but they also attack crops and can spread plant diseases. Some species live in small social colonies, defended by soldiers from predators and other thrips.

Thrips are cigar-shaped insects that are generally yellow, orange, dark brown, or black. They are between 0.03 and 0.1 inches (1 and 3 mm) long. Young thrips are white or yellow and look similar to the adults. The word *thrips* is both singular and plural—there is no such thing as a thrip. Like other insects, such as houseflies, thrips can walk on smooth surfaces, including glass, because they have a sticky pad on the tip of each foot, between the claws.

There are more than 4,500 species of thrips worldwide, with around 700 living in North America. The ancient ancestors of thrips probably lived among leaf litter on the forest floor, as many still do. Later, thrips diversified, and today many species live on leaves, fungi, and flowers, where they feed on pollen grains.

Classifying thrips

Thrips belong to the order Thysanoptera, which means "fringe-winged." This is because they have two pairs of narrow, featherlike wings that are fringed with hairs.

Scientists divide the thrips into two suborders. Terebrantids have short, pointed abdomens with sawlike ovipositors (egg tubes). The abdomens of the other group, tubuliferans, are long and narrow and do not have ovipositors.

Thrips are poor fliers, but they can be transported over long distances by storms and strong winds. This has earned thrips that live on corn and other cereals the common names of thunderbugs or thunderflies.

Laying eggs

Thrips spend the winter hiding in leaf litter or in sheltered parts of the host plant. In the spring, most thrips emerge from their shelters, and the females start

▲ *A thrips seen through a microscope. The wings are fringed with long hairs.*

laying eggs. Thrips eggs are large when compared to the size of the females' abdomens, so the females usually carry just a few eggs ready for laying at any one time. The eggs are kidney-shaped with delicate pale white or yellow shells. Terebrantids use their ovipositors to make tiny cuts into plants and lay single eggs inside. Tubuliferans lay their eggs on the surfaces of flowers, leaves, or fungi, in galls (swellings on plants), or in crevices in bark made by other insects.

Strange ways

After hatching, thrips development proceeds in a very unusual way. Although they are related to bugs, such as cicadas and aphids, thrips do not develop gradually by incomplete metamorphosis. Nor do these insects undergo complete metamorphosis and change dramatically from a larva into an adult, as do insects like bees and butterflies. Instead, the metamorphosis of thrips is somewhere between the two.

There are four stages, or instars, between the egg and the adult. At the end of each instar the insect molts (sheds its skin). During the first two stages, young thrips feed. The thrips do not feed during the third and

fourth instars, when they remain quite inactive. The duration of each instar depends on the temperature. In good conditions, there may be up to five generations of thrips every year.

Bizarre reproduction

Thrips reproduce in a very strange way. As in many insects, reproduction can take place without fertilization of the eggs by a male. This type of reproduction is called parthenogenesis, and in

▲ *An adult thrips resting on a leaf. These insects are often dispersed over long distances by strong winds, for which they are sometimes called thunderbugs.*

KEY FACTS

Name
Western flower thrips (*Frankliniella occidentalis*)

Distinctive features
Four wings fringed with long hairs

Breeding
Males compete by hitting each other with their abdomens, each trying to flick the other over

Size
Around 0.1 inches (3 mm) long

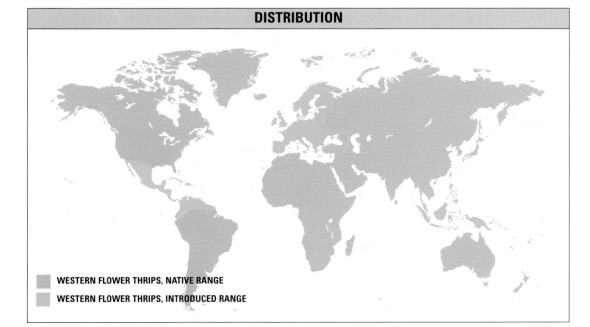

DISTRIBUTION

WESTERN FLOWER THRIPS, NATIVE RANGE
WESTERN FLOWER THRIPS, INTRODUCED RANGE

most insects it produces a population of female insects. However, in thrips, parthenogenesis results in male offspring, while reproduction with fertilization produces only female thrips.

Thrips defenses

Many animals prey on thrips, but these tiny insects have several defenses. Many species can secrete powerful toxins from their anuses (rear gut opening). Western flower thrips can detect the chemicals that some predatory bugs release as they feed. The thrips hide away in the silken nests of two-spotted spider mites, which feed on a similar range of plants. The hunting bugs cannot penetrate the dense tangle of silk to attack the thrips.

Several species of thrips are social, living inside galls (swellings) on the leaves of some types of acacia plants. Some of these thrips are soldiers that do not reproduce but live only to protect other members of the colony from attack. The soldier thrips often have large, spiny forelegs with which they battle marauding ants and thrips from other species that attempt to invade the gall. The invading thrips

Thrips, pollination, and the evolution of bees

Cycads are an ancient group of plants that first grew on Earth around 300 million years ago. Today, some cycads are pollinated by primitive species of thrips. The thrips live and breed inside the cycad cones, transferring pollen grains as they go. This suggests that thrips were involved in moving pollen from plant to plant long before the appearance of flowering plants, or angiosperms, which today are the main group of plants on land.

Thrips may have played an important role in the evolution of angiosperms. The movement of thrips inside male flowers of some palm trees triggers the release of plumes of pollen. Once airborne, the palm pollen drifts on the wind to female flowers, which are rarely visited by the insects. This is called insect-induced wind pollination. This may have been an important step between pollination that uses just the wind, seen today in plants such as pine trees and grasses, and the insect-based pollination of most angiosperms.

As angiosperms developed ways to attract insects to enter their flowers, insects such as bees and butterflies evolved, taking advantage of this new food source. Without thrips, flowering plants may never have evolved, and neither would have honeybees nor swallowtails.

sometimes have stout spines on their abdomens with which they attempt to eject the residents.

Some acacia thrips glue the leaves together to form a nest, using sticky chemicals secreted from their anuses. Safe from predators inside the nest, the thrips feed on the leaves.

▼ *Thrips pollinate many plants. The pollen sticks to their bodies as they feed and is transferred when the thrips move to other flowers.*

Economic pests

Many thrips are destructive pests of plants, especially grain crops, fruits, vegetables, and ornamental garden flowers. For example, the western flower thrips feeds on more than 500 different species of plants, many of them cultivated crops and flowers, including peppers, eggplants, cucumbers, watermelons, carnations, chrysanthemums, and orchids. Native to North America, the western flower thrips has spread to the Canary Islands, parts of Europe, Hawaii, New Zealand, and northern South America. These thrips cause damage to the plants by puncturing the leaves, flowers, or stems with their mandibles and then sucking up the sap through their tubelike mouthparts.

Leaves attacked by thrips usually appear silvery, and the undersides are spotted with small black specks before the leaves turn brown and die. Flowers become flecked, spotted, and misshapen, with many buds failing to open. Western flower thrips eat both flower petals and pollen. In addition

▲ *After one more molt, this young tubuliferan thrips will become an adult, able to fly and reproduce. This species lives inside flowers in the South American rain forest.*

SEE ALSO

- *Biological control*
- *Insect evolution*
- *Metamorphosis*
- *Pest*
- *Pollination*

to direct feeding damage, many plants die because this species of thrips carries a virus called tomato-spotted-wilttospovirus (TSWV). This virus attacks several important crops around the world. In Hawaii, TSWV has led to between 50 and 90 percent of the lettuce and tomato crops being lost.

Beneficial thrips

However, not all thrips are pests. Some are beneficial insects and may control predatory mites, small insects, and weeds. For example, the predatory six-spotted thrips is used in California as a biological control agent against the persea mite. This mite is native to Mexico and is a pest of a wide range of fruit and ornamental flowers, including avocados, peaches, apricots, and roses. Six-spotted thrips live within clusters of persea mites in late summer. They can be recognized by the six spots on the forewings. The thrips feed on the eggs, young, and adult mites, using their forelegs to hold and rotate their prey before piercing the soft underside of their bodies and feeding.

TICK AND MITE

Ticks and mites are small spiderlike creatures. Ticks suck blood, while mites eat a variety of foods and live in all sorts of places, from people's eyelashes to the throats of bees.

Together with their larger relatives ticks, mites make up one of the most widespread and successful groups of animals on Earth. The range of habitats these creatures have colonized is enormous. They live in deserts, rivers, lakes, ponds, grasslands, rain forests, temperate forests, caves, and even hot springs. They have been found halfway up Mount Everest, in the frozen wastes of Antarctica, and drifting along high in the atmosphere. Some species have adapted to live in very specific places, such as inside the throat of a honeybee

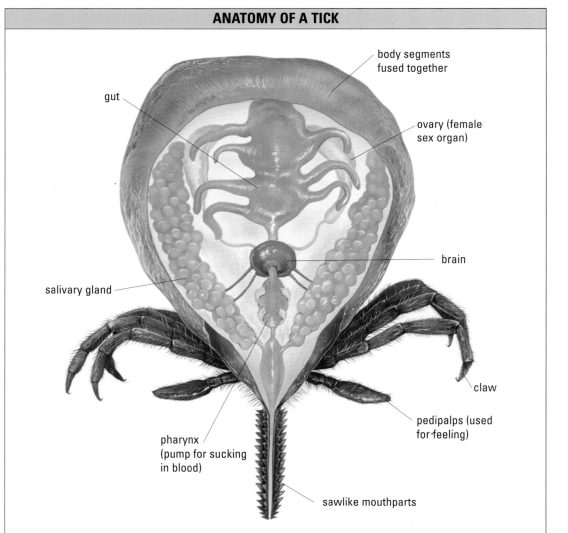

ANATOMY OF A TICK

gut

body segments fused together

ovary (female sex organ)

brain

salivary gland

claw

pedipalps (used for feeling)

pharynx (pump for sucking in blood)

sawlike mouthparts

◄ *The internal anatomy of a tick seen from above. The body of a tick can triple in size after feeding on blood.*

◄ *The head of a Rocky Mountain wood tick seen through a powerful microscope. The mouthparts are drawn inside the top of the head.*

KEY FACTS

Name
Rocky Mountain wood tick (*Dermacentor andersoni*)

Distinctive features
Carries disease-causing agents, such as Rocky Mountain spotted fever bacteria and Colorado tick fever virus

Habitat
Grassland and the edges of woods

Behavior
Sits at top of grass stalk and extends forelegs, climbing onto passing hosts

Feeding
Sucks mammal's blood for several days at a time

Breeding
Female lays many thousands of eggs

Life span
1 to 3 years

Size
Before eating: 0.08 to 0.23 inches (2 to 6 mm) long; after eating: 0.7 inches (17 mm) long

or in the holes in the roots of human eyelashes. Every person on Earth has mites living on their skin, mostly without any ill effects at all.

Spider cousins

Ticks and mites belong to the group of arthropods called the arachnids, which also includes spiders and scorpions. Mites are more common than spiders, but they are rarely noticed because most are smaller than a period. However, a few are larger—the giant velvet mite measures up to 0.6 inches (1.6 cm) long.

Ticks are easier to see, especially when they swell up after drinking blood from another animal. All ticks are blood-sucking parasites that feed on larger animals, including people.

Out for the count

Nobody knows how many species of ticks and mites there are. Scientists have described around 45,000 species, but the total is probably nearer one million.

Many of the best-known mites are parasites, feeding on the outside of larger host animals, but others eat plants, fungi, or rotting matter, and some are predators. Vast numbers of these arachnids live in soil and dirt, where they help recycle nutrients by eating the remains of dead organisms.

Scientists estimate that 3 square feet (1 sq m) of dead leaves on a forest floor harbors around one million mites of 200 different species. Most of these are beetle mites—tiny, beetlelike creatures that eat the leaves.

People's homes also teem with mites. The average bed contains hundreds of thousands of dust mites, which feed on the flecks of dead skin that continually fall from human bodies. These mites also infest carpets, furniture, and clothes. Many people are allergic to dust, which means they become short of breath and have a runny nose and watery eyes. The shed exoskeletons (skins) of mites may cause many of these allergies.

▲ *The dark object in the center of this bee pupa is a* Varroa *mite. These mites infect growing bees with a virus that can wipe out entire bee colonies. The mites are a major pest for beekeepers.*

Deadly ticks

A bite from a species of tick that lives in eastern Australia can kill a person. The saliva of the so-called paralysis tick contains a nerve poison that causes tiredness, blurred vision, and in extreme cases paralysis and death. Native Australian marsupials, such as quolls and bandicoots, are resistant to the ticks' poison, but pets, such as cats and dogs, and also small children are at risk from the effects of this tick.

Another dangerous disease associated by tick bites is human ehrlichiosis. This disease is caused by bacteria that can get into a person's blood when they are bitten by a deer tick, dog tick, or lone star tick. The bacteria attack white blood cells, producing fever, headaches, and sickness. Strong bacteria-killing medicines are needed to treat the disease, which is quite rare in the United States. However, there are occasional cases in cool, rural areas, such as New York State.

Body facts

The smallest mites grow to only about 0.004 inches (0.1 mm) long, which is too small to see with the naked eye, while the largest may reach up to 0.6 inches (16 mm) long. Compared to mites, ticks are giants, reaching 1.2 inches (30 mm) long after a meal.

Mature ticks and mites usually have eight legs, but their young generally have six. While spiders' bodies are divided into obvious front and back parts connected by a narrow waist, ticks and mites usually have oval bodies without waists.

The mouths of ticks and mites, like those of spiders, are flanked by two pairs of mouthparts. The front set, called chelicerae, are used as pincers or for piercing food. A few species of mites can swallow solid objects, such as fungal spores, but most mites and all ticks take in liquid food.

In species with piercing mouthparts, the chelicerae inject chemicals called enzymes into the food that turn it into a

DISTRIBUTION

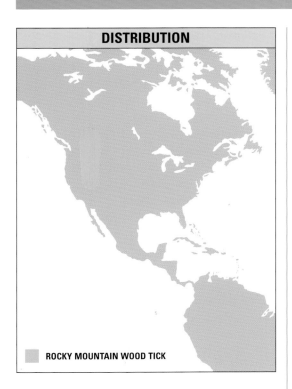

ROCKY MOUNTAIN WOOD TICK

nearest male grabs her with his legs, hauls her out of the mother, and mates with her immediately.

Most ticks and mites lay eggs after mating rather than giving birth to live young. The young that hatch from the eggs are miniature versions of the adults, but with fewer legs. They go through a series of molts as they develop into adults.

Pests

The best known ticks and mites are those that are a nuisance in some way. Red spider mites, for instance, are well known to gardeners because they often feed on greenhouse plants.

Mites that infest people's homes include the cheese mite, flour mite, and furniture mite, all of which are named for the food they eat, although the

▼ *An adult deer tick on a leaf. This type of tick transmits the microorganisms that cause Lyme disease.*

soupy liquid that is easy to suck up. The second pair of appendages are called pedipalps. Pedipalps are used as feelers, though some species grasp prey, pierce food, or spin silk with them.

Breeding systems

Ticks and mites mate in many different ways. Some species do not even need to mate. Females of these species lay unfertilized eggs that hatch into females.

The males of many mite species that do mate have a penislike sex organ for moving sperm into the female's body. Others use their legs or mouthparts to push sperm inside the female. Still other males simply leave their sperm in a packet on the ground for the female to collect. Male ticks use their mouthparts to widen the female's sexual opening, then they turn around and deposit a packet of sperm there.

Brothers and sisters

Perhaps the strangest mating behavior is that of the moth mite, which gives birth to sexually mature young. Newly born male moth mites wait by their mother's body for their sisters to be born. As soon as a female appears, the

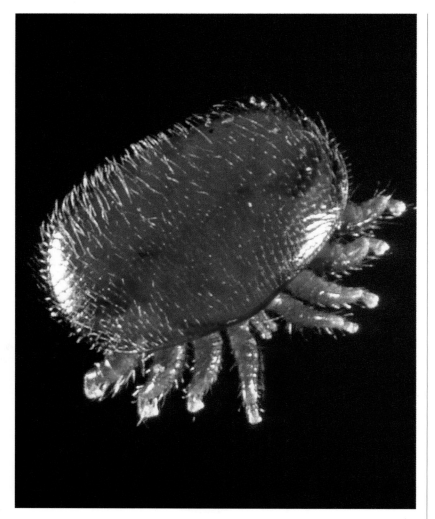

▲ *A close-up of an adult mite seen from above. The two central appendages are pedipalps; the other eight are the mite's legs.*

cheese mite also likes ham and bacon. Mites are most common in damp houses, where they can sometimes form crawling, dustlike masses.

Skin deep

The mites that live on a person's skin are called follicle mites. They usually live on the nose, forehead, and in the roots of eyelashes. They are also common in blackheads (pores blocked with dirt). Follicle mites do very little harm and may even help keep our skin clean, but other mites that live in the skin are less tolerable. For example, the scabies mite, also known as the itch mite, causes an itchy rash by burrowing through skin. Scabies mites are very common in furry animals, such as cats and dogs, where they cause a skin condition called mange, which makes the fur fall out.

Tick on and off

While parasitic mites often live entirely on one host, ticks only visit their hosts to feed. They can smell approaching animals with scent organs at the tips of their forelegs. When a suitable host approaches, a waiting tick climbs up a blade of grass or other plant and waves its front legs in the air to detect its victim. It drops onto the host's body as the animal brushes past.

Once aboard the host, the tick wriggles through the animal's fur and punctures the skin with its sharp mouthparts. These have sawlike edges that are difficult to pull out. The mouthparts hold the tick in place. Ticks may stay attached for several days while they swell up with blood. Some ticks can survive for up to three years between blood meals.

After feeding, they drop to the ground to molt or lay eggs. The six-legged young acquire their fourth pair of legs after their first molt but need to molt at least once more before becoming fully mature adults.

Tick facts

There are around 800 species of ticks, nearly all of which belong in two groups: hard ticks and soft ticks. Hard ticks are named for a thickened shield on the front of the body. Soft ticks have weaker mouthparts and feed on their hosts for only a few minutes at a time. This second group of ticks tends to live in their hosts' nests or burrows.

While ticks have names such as dog tick, deer tick, and sheep tick, all of these species will attack most land mammals, including people. Some ticks pass on disease-causing agents, such as viruses and bacteria, through their saliva. The Rocky Mountain wood tick can give people Rocky Mountain spotted fever, and the deer tick spreads Lyme disease. If someone gets bitten by a tick, he or she should pull it out by gripping its head with tweezers. Using just fingers may cause the tick's head to snap off and stay stuck in the skin.

TIGER BEETLE

Tiger beetles are fierce beetles that are easily recognized by their huge eyes and massive, sicklelike mouthparts.

Tiger beetles are usually brightly colored, and many have a metallic sheen. The elytra (wing cases) of most species have white markings around the edges. There are around 2,000 species of tiger beetles in the world, and about 150 of these live in North America. Tiger beetles live almost everywhere except Antarctica and some islands. They are most common in tropical parts of the world, and fewer live in cooler areas to the north and south.

Hunting life
Both adult and larval tiger beetles are predators. Females lay each of their eggs in individual tunnels, which they dig out of soil. When a larva hatches from an egg, it makes the tunnel larger and sits near the mouth, waiting for prey, such as ants or small flies, to pass by outside. As the larva grows, it makes the burrow larger and deeper—up to 6 feet (2 m) deep in some cases.

The body of a tiger beetle larva is well adapted for life underground. It has a flat head and pronotum (shieldlike plate behind the head), which it uses to plug the entrance of its burrow. The larva hangs inside the tunnel, held in place by a hooklike structure on the back of the abdomen. When prey passes by the burrow, the larva strikes rapidly with its massive mouthparts, dragging

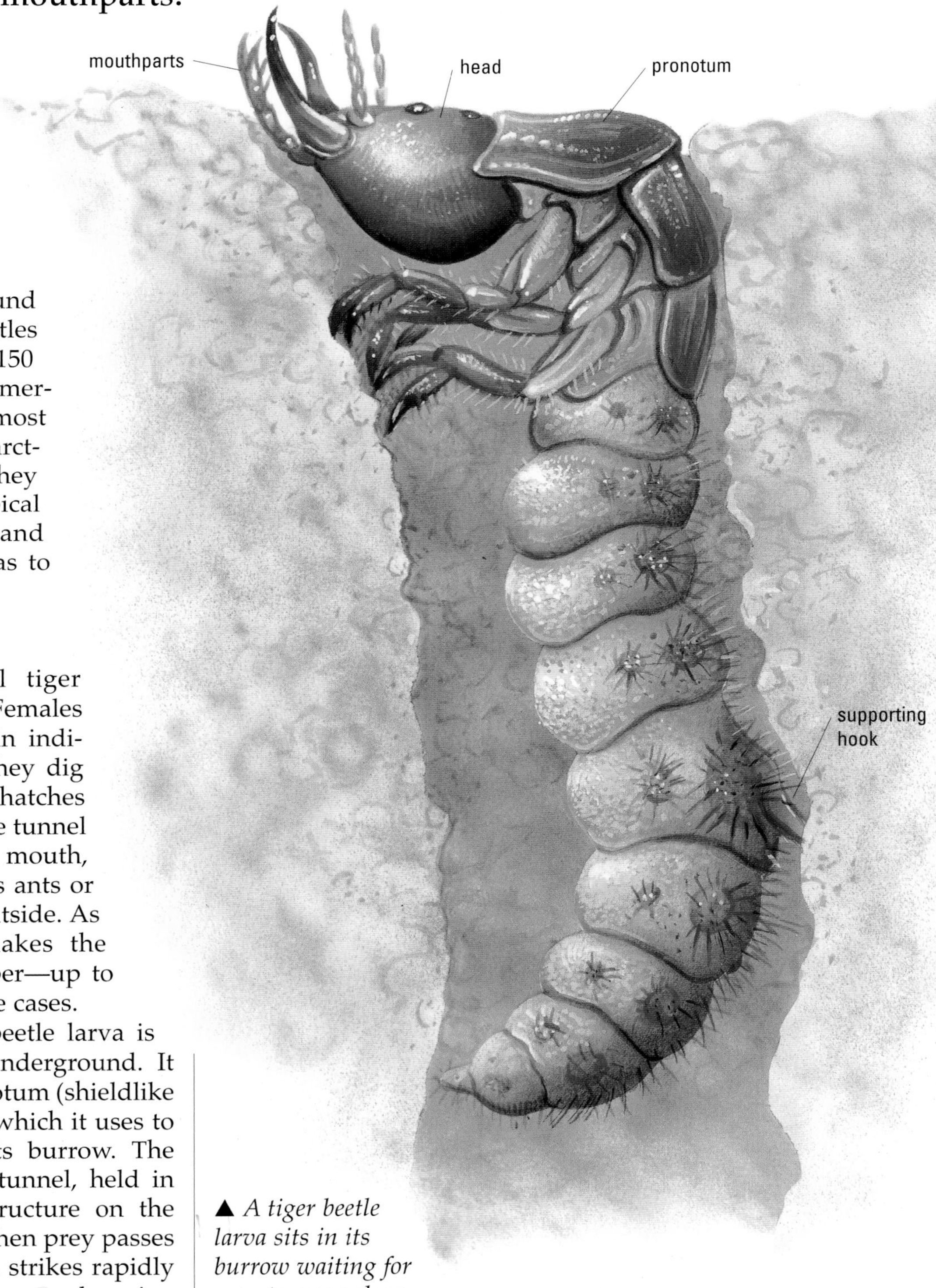

mouthparts

head

pronotum

supporting hook

▲ *A tiger beetle larva sits in its burrow waiting for prey to come along.*

▲ *A tiger beetle's large eyes and huge mouthparts help it find and kill prey.*

KEY FACTS

Name
Coastal tiger beetle (*Cicindela dorsalis dorsalis*)

Distinctive features
White elytra with bronze lines; white hairs behind head

Distribution
Atlantic coast of United States

Size
0.6 inches (14 mm)

▶ *A male (top) and female tiger beetle mating.*

SEE ALSO

- *Beetle*
- *Ground beetle*

the prey back into the burrow. The larva's strike takes less than 0.03 seconds. A tiger beetle larva hunts like this for up to three years before pupating in the burrow.

Adult life

Unlike the larvae, which lie in wait for prey to pass by, adult tiger beetles are active, agile hunters with excellent eyesight. They are also the fastest-running insects in the world. Biologists have recorded one Australian species running at up to 5.6 miles per hour (9 km/h) over short distances.

Some rare tropical species live on moss-covered rocks in cold, fast-moving streams. Other tropical tiger beetles live in trees, where they hunt through the branches and leaves. Some tiger beetles, such as the coastal tiger beetle, live in sandy areas. This species has become very rare due to human activity in their beach habitat.

Hunting habits

Most species of tiger beetles are active during the day and prefer open, sunny areas, often taking cover when the Sun is covered by clouds. There are some species that are nocturnal (active at night). Nocturnal tiger beetles usually have black bodies, cannot fly, and tend to be larger than the species that are active during the day.

Tiger beetles have few predators due to their agility and speed. There are, however, a number of other insects that are parasites of tiger beetle larvae. These include some bee fly larvae, and several species of tiny parasitic wasps.

TIGER MOTH

A large and varied group of moths, tiger moths and their relatives live all over the world. While the adults are admired for their colorful wings, the caterpillars are well known for their hairy bodies.

Tiger moths belong to a family of moths called the Arctiidae. As well as tiger moths, this family also includes a group known as ermine moths and another called footman moths.

Together, these moths make up one of the largest moth families, with as many as 10,000 species known across the world. In general, the moths in this family have stout and hairy bodies. Tiger and ermine moths have broad wings, whereas those of footman moths are more slender.

Color patterns

Tiger moths are brightly colored, but ermines tend to be white, with darker spots and patches. Footmen moths are duller in color. The garden tiger has characteristic red and brown hind wings and abdomen, with brown and white forewings and head. Its relative, the virgin tiger, has a very similar coloration, and the pattern warns potential predators that the adult is unpleasant to eat. By contrast, the white ermine is mainly white, decorated with a few dark spots. However, this species' red abdomen also acts as a warning to predators.

Hairy larvae

Though many of the adults in this family of moths look different from each other, the caterpillars have much in common. The caterpillars' bodies are all quite stout and are covered in many hairs.

The hairs of the caterpillars serve a defensive function. They irritate the mouth and intestines of predators, such as birds, so the caterpillars are spat out and not eaten again. The hairs are long and have many tiny bristles that help irritate. This protection is so effective that the silk cocoons used by tiger moth pupae also contain these hairs.

Look-alikes

The cinnabar moth is a strikingly colored black and red moth that looks similar to a number of burnet

◄ *A garden tiger moth, with its brightly colored wings and body, is typical of most tiger moths. The colors warn predators that the moth tastes bad.*

KEY FACTS

Name
Garden tiger
(*Arctia caja*)

Distinctive features
Abdomen and hind wings are orange and brown; fore-wings have white stripes; larva has irritating hairs

Size
Wingspan: 2 to 3 inches (5 to 7.5 cm)

SEE ALSO

- *Gypsy moth*
- *Moth and butterfly*
- *Owlet moth*

▼ *This dogbane tiger moth caterpillar is covered in protective hairs.*

moths, which belong to another family. Both the burnets and the cinnabar moth are poisonous, and by having similar coloration, they reinforce the association of their colors with their unpleasantness for predators. The caterpillars of the cinnabar moth also have warning coloration of bright orange and brown bands. They feed only on ragwort plants, using the plants' poisons for their own protection.

Jamming signals

Bats are important predators of tiger moths. Bats find their way and hunt in the dark by bouncing bursts of sound off objects. They listen to the echoes to find out how large and far away things are—this is called echolocation. Some tiger moths are able to produce their own bursts of sound that interfere with the echolocation signals, helping the moths avoid the bats.

Feeding time

Tiger moths feed on a wide range of plants, depending on species. Some feed on plants such as dock; others on tropical vines. The adult females deposit their eggs on these plants, so the cater-

DISTRIBUTION

■ WATER TIGER

pillars can start to feed as soon as they hatch. Water tigers, however, are different. The larvae feed on a range of aquatic (water-living) plants. The dense hairs of the caterpillar trap a layer of air around the body. This air layer allows the caterpillar to breathe while submerged beneath the surface.

TRAP-DOOR SPIDER

With the doors to their burrows slightly ajar, trap-door spiders ambush insects that pass close by. The burrow entrances are well camouflaged, and females may live inside for many years.

Trap-door spiders are related to tarantulas and funnel-web spiders. All these spiders share several features, including fangs that are hinged to move up and down instead of side to side, as in other spiders, and two pairs of book lungs. Trap-door spiders belong to the family Ctenizidae and are common in southern Africa, Asia, Australia, Europe, and the Americas.

Fifteen species live in the United States, most of which are found in the southern and western states. Like tarantulas, trap-door spiders take several years to mature, and females live longer than males. Trap-door spiders are difficult to find because they live in burrows concealed by a hinged, camouflaged lid that opens like a trapdoor.

Spotting trap-door spiders

Female trap-door spiders very rarely leave their burrows. Males are often seen, especially after heavy rains, as they wander in search of mates. Trap-door spiders are usually shiny brown or black and may reach up to one inch (25 mm) long. Female spiders are

◀ *A tree trunk trap-door spider. The door to its burrow (left) is open and camouflaged with lichen from the tree trunk.*

559

Thick, pluglike
trapdoor

Trap-door
spider detects
vibrations
through hairs
on its legs

The grasshopper
is seized and
injected with
venom

◄ *Capturing prey the trap-door spider way. This California trap-door spider detects vibrations through the soil caused by a grasshopper. When the insect is in range, the spider swiftly grabs it, bites it, and retreats back to the safety of the tunnel to feed.*

larger than males, which are often mistaken for young, shiny tarantulas as they wander about in search of female burrows. The male's legs are longer and more slender than those of the females.

Digging burrows

Female trap-door spiders spend most of their lives in burrows dug 4 to 10 inches (10 to 25 cm) straight into the ground. The burrows are usually no more than 0.5 inches (13 mm) wide, though there is enough space for the spider to turn around inside. The spiders use a series of spines on their chelicerae (mouthparts), called a rastellum, to cut through the soil, which is carried to the surface for disposal. The fangs are used to smooth the insides of the burrow, after which the spider lines the walls with thick sheets of velvety silk.

Many species of trap-door spiders use some of the soil to mold a thick, pluglike door, reinforced with silk. These doors have slanted edges that fit snugly into the entrance to the burrow. Other spiders make a silky, wafer-thin door, which fits more loosely into the entrance hole.

The door is covered with pieces of soil and lichen (fungi and algae living together) and is camouflaged when closed. Some spiders hold their doors shut by gripping them with their fangs and pushing against the walls of the burrow with their legs. One species holds the door with its front legs, leaving the fangs free to strike out at intruders.

Pouncing on prey

When night falls, the trap-door spider lifts the door slightly and stretches out its front legs. Some species detect the vibrations of insects and other small arthropods as they walk overhead. Others wait for prey to come into contact with the legs, or to actually blunder into the door. Once the prey is detected and is in range, the spider

DISTRIBUTION

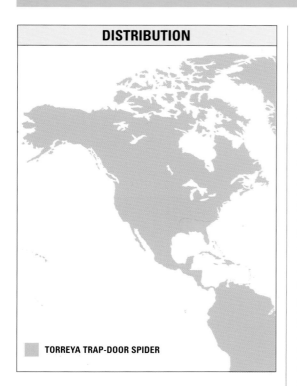

TORREYA TRAP-DOOR SPIDER

pounces, then returns to the safety of the burrow just as swiftly. The spider usually keeps its hind legs in contact with the burrow, but some will pursue prey for a short distance.

An early-warning system

To improve the chances of detecting prey, some trap-door spiders surround the doors to their burrows with a fan of silk tripwires. The spider keeps its front legs in contact with the tripwires. However, spider silk is an energetically expensive material to manufacture. A number of Australian species economize by arranging a series of twigs around the entrances to their burrows. Short sections of silk at the ends inform the spider if an insect wanders over one of the twigs.

Mating and reproduction

After summer rains, each mature male trap-door spider abandons its burrow and begins to search for a mate. They are guided by an attractant chemical, or pheromone, released by the female. When a male locates the burrow of a female, he signals to her before entering by tapping on the lid with his front legs.

The spiders mate inside the burrow, and then the male leaves. The female seals the lid before laying 200 to 300 eggs in a silken sac. After molting, the young spiderlings strike out on their own to construct their own burrows.

Enemies of trap-door spiders

The burrows of trap-door spiders are camouflaged and hard to find. However, their main enemies, spider-hunting wasps, use chemical cues to find their well-hidden quarry. Female wasps either lift up or chew through the lid before they sting the spider and lay a single egg on its paralyzed body. The spider becomes food for a wasp larva. Many trap-door spiders seem defenseless against these insects, but some can protect themselves. For example, when disturbed, a Torreya trap-door spider runs headfirst down its burrow, wedging its flat, grooved abdomen against the sides. The flat rear of the abdomen is covered in tough armor, which the wasp cannot get through. Other spiders dig side tunnels off the main burrow as escape routes.

Trap-door spiders are attacked by other parasites, such as small-headed flies, while skunks, raccoons, and coatis dig up and eat trap-door spiders.

SEE ALSO

- *Funnel-web spider*
- *Parasitic fly*
- *Parasitic wasp*
- *Senses*
- *Spider*
- *Tarantula*

▼ *A trap-door spider waits for prey to wander into range. This species builds a thick pluglike door that fits snugly into the entrance of the burrow.*

TSETSE FLY

The bloodsucking tsetse fly is one of the most dangerous insects in Africa. A single bite from this fly can lead to the deadly disease sleeping sickness.

Tsetse flies are found only in Africa between the Sahara and Kalahari Deserts. The flies breed in wooded areas, so the deserts act as barriers to their spread, confining the flies to the central, tropical part of Africa. There, they feast on the blood of people and many other animals.

As they feed, tsetse flies spread the microorganisms that cause sleeping sickness, a disease that can kill people and domestic animals. Because of this disease, raising cattle and other domestic animals in some parts of Africa is impossible. While this has prevented farmers from turning Africa's natural wilderness areas into ranches, the disease has also meant that many of the local people live in poverty.

Body facts
Tsetse flies look very much like their close relative the housefly, but at 0.25 to 0.6 inches (6 to 16 mm) long, they are slightly larger. The flies vary in color from yellow to dark brown, with a gray thorax (midbody) and sometimes a pattern of bands on the abdomen.

▲ *A tsetse fly feeding on human blood. The insect's abdomen is swollen with the developing larva.*

Whereas houseflies have spongelike mouthparts for sucking fluid from soggy food, tsetse flies have piercing mouthparts to penetrate the skins of the animal they feed on. They normally hold their mouthparts next to the body but flex them downward before biting.

Fly types

There are about 20 species of tsetse flies, each of which lives in a particular type of environment. Some thrive only in moist tropical rain forests, while others prefer forest fringes or savanna, that are dotted with just a few trees. Tsetse flies seldom venture far into open grassland, except to attack animals near enough to see. The adult flies feed on blood from a variety of animals, including large mammals such as antelopes, people, and cattle, as well as birds, crocodiles, and other reptiles.

Breeding behavior

All tsetse species breed in the same way. Unusually for an insect, the females produce only one offspring at a time. The egg hatches inside the female's body, where the larva develops inside a uterus. The larva feeds on a milklike substance secreted by the uterus wall. The adult female must obtain a blood meal to produce a healthy larva; otherwise, it will be too small and weak to

KEY FACTS

Name
Tsetse flies
(genus *Glossina*)

Distinctive features
Piercing mouthparts and bristles on antennae

Habitat
African woodlands

Breeding
Single larva
born alive

Size
0.25 to 0.6 inches
(6 to 16 mm) long

SEE ALSO

- *Blackfly*
- *Disease carrier*
- *Fly*
- *Horsefly*
- *Housefly*
- *Warble fly and botfly*

▼ *A female tsetse fly gives birth to her single larva.*

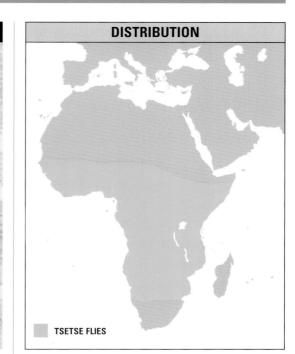

DISTRIBUTION

☐ **TSETSE FLIES**

survive when it is born. After about nine days of growth inside the adult female, the larva is ready to pupate. The female searches out a shady area under a tree and gives birth on the ground where the earth is soft. The larva wriggles into the soil and forms a pupa within an hour or so. After several weeks of development, a new adult emerges.

Silent killers

Tsetse flies are most active during the warmest part of the day. Both male and female flies feed on blood. They use their sense of sight to locate prey and then smell their way to a good part of the body to bite into.

Two species of tsetse flies transmit the organism that causes sleeping sickness in people. The tiny organism is called a trypanosome. The trypanosomes multiply in the blood, causing fever, and they eventually spread to the brain and heart, both of which may become damaged permanently. The disease is named for the attacks of intense sleepiness that affect sufferers even in the middle of the day. Without treatment, a person with sleeping sickness will become dazed, before the victim falls into a coma (sleeplike state) and dies.

TUMBU FLY

With larvae that feast on the flesh of humans, dogs, and other animals, tumbu flies are common throughout central Africa.

◀ *Two tumbu fly larvae that have been removed from a person's skin.*

KEY FACTS

Name
Tumbu fly
(*Cordylobia anthropophaga*)

Distinctive features
Yellow, red, and brown blowfly

Breeding
Female lays 200 to 300 eggs in a single batch

Food
Larva feeds on host's tissue and pus

Distribution
In Africa, south of the Sahara Desert

Size
0.5 inches (12 mm) long once adult

Adult tumbu flies are large blowflies that measure up to 0.5 inches (12 mm) long. They live in Africa, south of the Sahara Desert. Unlike other blowflies, adult tumbu flies' bodies do not have a metallic shine. Instead, they are a dull yellow-brown or red-brown.

Flesh-eating larvae

The female lays her eggs on the ground in batches of 200 or 300. The eggs hatch in a couple of days, and the larvae stay hidden beneath the surface of the soil, without feeding, for up to 15 days. However, if they sense a rise in temperature, vibrations in the soil, or carbon dioxide (the gas breathed out by animals), the larvae quickly wriggle to the surface, as these signals show that an animal is nearby. If an animal is present, the larvae burrow into the skin.

Each larva does not burrow around under the skin but forms a swelling that has a hole at the end so it can breathe. It feeds on the host's body tissue for around one or two weeks, during which time it grows along with the swelling. The larva can reach 0.6 inches (15 mm) long and has stout spines that prevent it from being dragged from the swelling easily. When the larva is fully grown, it bursts from the swelling, falls to the ground, and pupates. The adult fly emerges soon after.

Ironed out

Many animals are attacked by tumbu flies; among the most common are dogs and rats. Flies also lay eggs on drying clothes and the larvae then burrow into the wearer's skin. In west Africa, clothes are ironed to kill any tumbu fly larvae.

SEE ALSO

- *Blowfly and bluebottle*
- *Fly*
- *Warble fly and botfly*

TWISTED-WING PARASITE

A very unusual group, twisted-wing parasites live inside the bodies of other types of insects. The females never leave their hosts, while the males fly off to find mates. The males' twisted forewings give the group its name.

Twisted-wing parasites are a small group of unusual insects that are adapted to live inside other types of insects. The males and females lead remarkably different lives. Adult males are free-flying and measure less than 0.15 inches (4 mm) long. They have thin, fan-shaped hind wings, but their forewings are twisted into small stumps, for which the group are named. The stumps help the twisted-wing parasites balance during flight. The head of the male bears a pair of bulging eyes with large individual facets (lenses). Female twisted-wing parasites look very different. These insects spend the whole of their lives inside the bodies of their hosts, and are grublike, with few external features.

Host of changes

Twisted-wing parasites are hard to spot. There are only 550 species known throughout the world, 56 of which live in North America.

All twisted-wing parasites spend at least some of their lives inside another type of insect. Once infected with a twisted-wing parasite, the development of a host insect may begin to slow down. The host may also grow new features, and some even begin to look like members of the opposite sex. Infected insects can sometimes be spotted because part of the female twisted-wing parasites' bodies sticks out through the exoskeleton (skin) of the host.

A wide range of insect groups provide hosts for twisted-wing parasites. These hosts include thrips, grasshoppers, bugs, flies, ants, bees, and wasps.

▼ A male twisted-wing parasite seen through a very powerful microscope. The colors have been added using a computer.

forewing

eye facets

hind wing

565

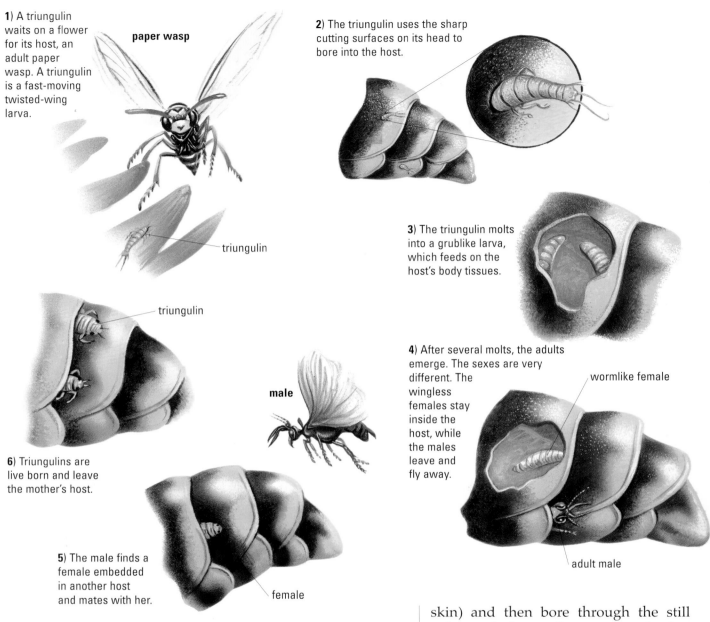

1) A triungulin waits on a flower for its host, an adult paper wasp. A triungulin is a fast-moving twisted-wing larva.

paper wasp

triungulin

2) The triungulin uses the sharp cutting surfaces on its head to bore into the host.

3) The triungulin molts into a grublike larva, which feeds on the host's body tissues.

triungulin

4) After several molts, the adults emerge. The sexes are very different. The wingless females stay inside the host, while the males leave and fly away.

wormlike female

male

6) Triungulins are live born and leave the mother's host.

5) The male finds a female embedded in another host and mates with her.

female

adult male

▲ *The life cycle of twisted-wing parasites.*

Life on the outside

The twisted-wing parasite life cycle is complex. The first larval stage is called a triungulin. Unlike the larvae of many insects, triungulins are not slow-moving and wormlike. Instead, they have legs and are very active.

The triungulins are live born, and they seek out and attach themselves to a host as soon as possible. Some species enter the host immediately, burrowing through gaps in the exoskeleton. Other twisted-wing parasites wait on the outside until the host molts (sheds its skin) and then bore through the still soft exoskeleton. Some twisted-wing parasites ride with adult bees or wasps back to their nests, where the parasites attack the softer-bodied larvae.

Back inside

The triungulin bores into the host using sharp edges on its the head rather than its mouthparts. Soon after entering the host, the triungulin molts into a second stage, which is legless and wormlike and much better adapted for living inside another animal. The developing larva molts several more times inside the body of the host.

Twisted sisters

Twisted-wing parasites do not feed on host tissues. Instead, they drink the host's hemolymph (blood). Adult females are larviform—they look like larvae, but they have sexual organs. The adult female's abdomen embeds into the body of the host, and her head and thorax (midbody) stick out from the host's abdomen.

By contrast, adult males emerge from the pupal stage with wings. They struggle free from the host before flying off to mate with a female living inside another insect. They are short-lived, and must find a female quickly before they die.

Complex development

The complex metamorphosis of twisted-wing parasites is called hypermetamorphosis since it involves a number of different body forms. Hypermetamorphosis allows a developing insect to undertake several different ways of life. For example, if the insect larva needs to roam around to find a suitable host, a mobile triungulin form is best suited for this activity. However, a triungulin is not well suited to living inside another animal. Therefore, the triungulin soon molts into a second larval stage. This stage is grublike and legless to help it burrow through the tissues of the host. In addition to twisted-wing parasites, several other insects go through hypermetamorphosis, including some thrips and a few beetles, such as blister beetles.

The differences between the sexes also reflect their different lifestyles. Female twisted-wing parasites do not need to leave their hosts and so do not waste energy developing legs and wings. However, males need to disperse and search for females and so they are free-living and mobile.

SEE ALSO
- *Blister beetle*
- *Fly*
- *Metamorphosis*

▼ *A highly magnified* Eoxenos *triungulin boring into the exoskeleton of its host, a silverfish. The color has been added using a computer.*

VAMPIRE ANT

An unusual species of ant that drinks the hemolymph (blood) of its own young has shown scientists how ants may have evolved from wasps.

In 2000, biologists working in the forests of central Madagascar discovered a colony of very unusual reddish-brown ants. When the scientists examined these ants closely, they saw that this species shares more similarities with wasps than other ants do. Scientists think that ants and wasps evolved from the same type of insect around 100 million years ago.

Other ants have abdomens that are connected to the thorax (midbody) via a series of slender segments called a pedicel. This narrow waist gives the ants great flexibility. The newly discovered ants have just one joint between thorax and abdomen, the same arrangement as wasps. Scientists believe that the new species is very similar to the earliest ants that evolved.

Drinking children's blood
The scientists saw that the newly discovered ants also behaved in a very unusual way. Like other ants, the new species lives in large colonies, with workers foraging on the forest floor for

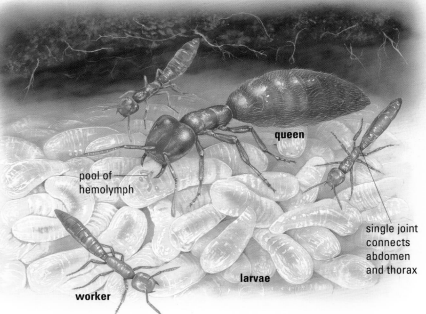

food to feed to the larvae. However, the foragers do not appear to supply food to other ants in the colony.

In order to feed, the queen bites a small hole in the outer skin of a larva. She then drinks from the small pool of hemolymph (blood) that oozes out. Scientists have called the ants vampire, or Dracula ants because of their unusual feeding habits. Remarkably, the larvae seem to be completely unaffected.

Other ant species feed their larvae solid food. The larvae partly digest the food before regurgitating it. The liquid is then given to other ants in the colony. This feeding behavior may have evolved from the hemolymph drinking seen in vampire ants.

The woods and forests of Madagascar are being chopped down at an alarming rate. Without urgent action, vampire ants and many other animals unique to Madagascar will disappear forever.

▲ *A queen vampire ant drinking hemolymph from one of her larvae. Workers feed the larvae with small pieces of prey, generally other insects that are captured outside the nest.*

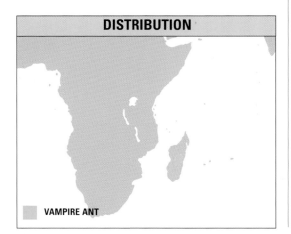

DISTRIBUTION

█ VAMPIRE ANT

SEE ALSO
- *Ant*
- *Insect evolution*
- *Social insect*

VELVET ANT

Although they look like large, fluffy ants, velvet ants are in fact wasps without wings. These brightly colored insects can give very painful stings.

Velvet ants are so named because the wingless females, with their covering of soft, velvety hair, are often mistaken for ants. However, velvet ants belong to a family of wasps. There are around 5,000 species of velvet ants worldwide, and 500 species live in North America. All are brightly colored and all are parasites of other insects.

The cow killer
A species of velvet ant common in the United States is also called the cow killer or mule killer because many people think that the female's sting is so powerful that it can kill a large animal. This is not true. While the sting is extremely painful and unpleasant, it does not usually cause serious harm to domestic animals or humans, except possibly in people who are allergic.

The female cow killer is between 0.5 inches and 1 inch (1.3 and 2.5 cm) long and does not have wings. Her body is black, but the top of her thorax (midbody) and abdomen are covered with bright red hairs. She has a stinger that can be up to half her body length and that is very flexible, so she can sting from almost any position. A female cow

▲ A female velvet ant walking across the ground. She does not have wings, and her body is toughened to fight off insects underground.

DISTRIBUTION

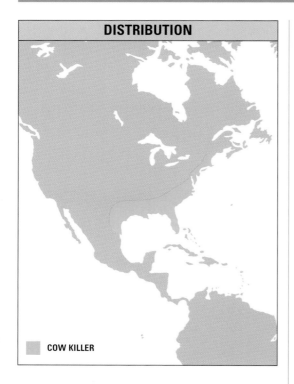

COW KILLER

suitable place to lay their eggs. Cow killers are parasites of bumblebees, and once a female has found a nest, she fights her way inside.

A female cow killer's exoskeleton (outer skin) is very thick and tough, protecting her from the stings of the defending bees. Once inside, the female looks for mature pupae. The velvet ant chews holes in the cells containing the pupae and lays an egg next to each bee pupa. Finally, she seals the cells up again with saliva.

When the velvet ant egg hatches, the larva feeds on the bee pupa. Within a few days, it completely consumes its victim and prepares to pupate itself. Depending on the time of year, the new adult velvet ant might either emerge to breed that same season or spend the winter in the bees' nest before emerging the following year.

SEE ALSO

- *Bumblebee*
- *Parasitic wasp*
- *Spider wasp*
- *Wasp*
- *Yellow jacket*

KEY FACTS

Name
Cow killer
(*Dasymutilla occidentalis*)

Distinctive features
Female is brightly colored and wingless; male is larger, darker, and has wings

Food
Adult: nectar; larva: bee pupa

Size
0.6 to 1 inch (16 to 25 mm) long

killer spends the day wandering on the ground, looking for a bumblebees' nest in which to lay her eggs.

Male cow killers look very different from the females. The males are larger but less colorful than the females. They have wings but do not have stingers. Most people would not recognize male cow killers as members of the same species as the females.

The cow killer is found mainly in the southern and eastern United States, from New York to Florida, and around the Gulf of Mexico to Texas. This insect prefers hot, dry areas such as desert, scrubland, and beaches, but also lives in meadows and on the edges of forests. The adults feed mainly on nectar. Although they are mainly active in the daytime, they shelter under leaves or debris when the sun is at its hottest.

Mating

Male cow killers fly low over the ground, searching for females, which they identify by scent. After mating just once the males die, but the females immediately begin searching for a

◀ *A female red velvet ant. These wasps are common in dry desert areas of the western United States.*

VELVET WORM

Velvet worms share many characteristics with both worms and arthropods. Their long, thin bodies look like worms, but like arthropods, they shed their skin and have claws.

Velvet worms are grouped separately from all other animals. They are grouped together as Onychophora, which means "claw bearing." Velvet worms are of great interest to biologists because they seem to be closely related to both arthropods and worms.

Velvet worms are mostly active at night, when the air is cool and moist. They walk on stumpy, clawed legs, extending and contracting their bodies from head to tip in much the same way an earthworm crawls through dirt.

Velvet worms appeared around 550 million years ago. These ancient animals lived in the ocean. One of the earliest, *Aysheaia*, is thought to have fed on sponges. However, all of today's velvet worms live on land. There are around 130 species worldwide. These are distinguished by the number of legs present, where the reproductive organs are, and by their colors.

Distribution and habitat

Velvet worms are divided into two groups. One family lives close to the equator in central America, Africa, and Southeast Asia. The other family lives in Chile, Australasia, and South Africa.

▼ *The striking blue color of this velvet worm may be used to display to other velvet worms or as a warning to predators.*

▶ *A velvet worm defends itself against a giant centipede. The velvet worm produces a sticky liquid that shoots out of appendages on either side of its mouthparts.*

velvet worm

centipede

Many animals, such as insects, can close the holes in their bodies through which they breathe to prevent losing water. Velvet worms cannot do this, and so they must live in wet areas. Most species live on the damp floor of tropical forests. However, one South African species lives in grasslands and escapes dry weather by squeezing its body into cracks in rocks and under soil.

Harsh New Zealand winters drive velvet worms underground for up to three months a year. Two blind species of velvet worms from Jamaica and South Africa live in underground caves throughout their lives.

Body plan

The wormlike bodies of velvet worms are protected by a thin elastic exoskeleton (outer covering) covered with bumps. The bumps are clothed with tiny scales, giving these animals their velvety appearance. Larger bumps are tipped by a single sensory bristle that velvet worms use to feel their surroundings. Velvet worms breathe through holes called spiracles. The air passes along tubes, or tracheae, inside the body to the worms' internal organs.

The head carries a pair of soft antennae. A small eye is positioned at the base of each antenna. The mouth has a pair of clawlike mouthparts and a rough tongue that grinds food.

Velvet worms' stubby legs do not have joints like arthropods' limbs do. The number of pairs of legs varies from 14 to 43, depending upon the age, sex, and species of velvet worm. Each leg has a pair of claws and three to six pads upon which the velvet worm walks.

Most full-grown velvet worms are 0.5 to 6 inches (1.3 to 15 cm) long. The females are generally larger than the males. The world's largest velvet worm, a species living in Costa Rica, measures 8 inches (20 cm) long. Velvet worms can be a variety of colors, including black, blue, red, brown, or gray.

◄ *A velvet worm capturing a cricket with threads of sticky spit. The threads dry and make it impossible for the prey to escape.*

A worm or an arthropod?

Velvet worms share many features with both worms and arthropods. Like worms, velvet worms have soft, flexible bodies with many repeating body segments, most of which contain organs that remove waste from the body. Neither of these groups have jointed legs, and they have just simple eyes.

However, velvet worms also have a lot in common with arthropods. Their skins contain chitin, a tough substance found in all insects, spiders, and other arthropods. Velvet worms must shed their skins to grow, just like insects. Velvet worms also have an open blood system, in which their hemolymph, or blood, flows into a central body cavity rather than traveling around through tubes.

Velvet worms get oxygen to their cells through a system of tubes called tracheae, just like insects. All arthropods have segmented limbs, and although velvet worms do not have limbs like these, their legs are similar in other ways. Their legs carry claws and, like arthropods, their mouthparts have evolved from legs.

◄ *A young velvet worm is born head first. Velvet worms are usually born in pairs.*

Life and death

Velvet worms are predators that slowly stalk small snails, insects, pill bugs, and true worms. Several species hunt for termites inside tunnels in rotten wood. Velvet worms capture their prey by spraying them with a sticky fluid squirted from their mouthparts. The fluid is a slimy mixture of proteins and water that dries quickly.

The mating behavior of velvet worms has not been studied in detail. The females of one Caribbean species can reproduce by parthenogenesis—without mating with a male—and no males of this species have been found. However, females of most species must mate before they can produce young.

A few Australian species lay eggs after mating. They use an egg-laying tube to deposit eggs in moist soil, dead leaves, or rotting logs. Other velvet worms keep their eggs inside the body until they hatch. The young of most species, however, develop and grow safe inside their mothers' bodies. The females feed their developing young through a placenta (an organ that is also found in most mammals and some sharks) for up to 15 months. The birth takes about an hour, and the young can soon use their sticky secretions for hunting prey and to defend themselves.

Velvet worms molt every two weeks. They reach their maximum size in about three or four years and live for up to six years. Males mature faster than females.

Friend or foe

Birds, snakes, fish, spiders, and large centipedes feed on velvet worms. When attacked, velvet worms spit two streams of sticky liquid. Larger species can spit almost 20 inches (50 cm). The streams harden quickly, trapping smaller attackers in a net of sticky threads. The brown color of many species helps them blend in among the leaves of the forest floor and avoid being spotted by predators.

Velvet worms are important in biological research. The study of these unique animals helps answer questions about

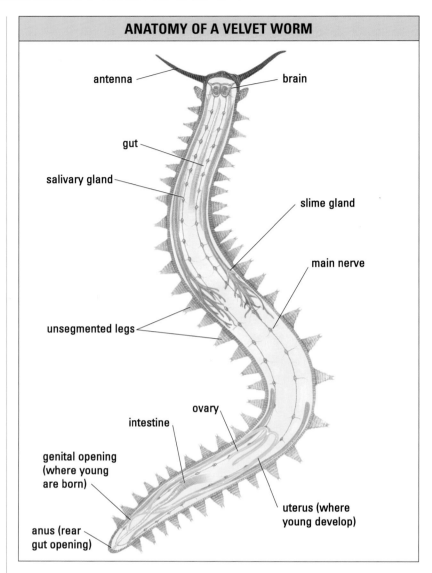

ANATOMY OF A VELVET WORM

antenna
brain
gut
salivary gland
slime gland
main nerve
unsegmented legs
ovary
intestine
genital opening (where young are born)
uterus (where young develop)
anus (rear gut opening)

▲ *The internal anatomy of a female velvet worm.*

SEE ALSO
- *Anatomy and physiology*
- *Arthropod*
- *Defense*
- *Insect evolution*
- *Spitting spider*

the evolution of arthropods. The modern distributions of velvet worms are also studied to help track movements of the continents over millions of years. The sticky spit of velvet worms might one day be used to seal cuts during microsurgery.

The International Union for the Conservation of Nature and Natural Resources (IUCN) lists several velvet worm species as vulnerable. Their populations are small and their habitats are being disturbed by human activities. Only in South Africa and Australia is it illegal to collect and sell velvet worms. However, local wildlife laws protect a few species from national parks and reserves in other parts of the world.

GLOSSARY

abdomen: the rear body section of insects, spiders, and other arthropods

alate: a winged adult insect of a species, such as an aphid, that also has adults without wings

antennae (an-TEH-nee): sensitive jointed feelers on the heads of insects

arthropod (AHR-thruh-PAHD): animal with several pairs of jointed limbs and a hard outer covering (exoskeleton)

cephalothorax (SEH-fuh-luh-THOR-AKS): the fused head and thorax of a spider

chelicerae (kih-LIH-suh-ree): appendages near an arachnid's mouth; those of spiders carry fangs

chrysalis (KRIH-suh-luhs): pupa of a butterfly

commensalism (kuh-MEN-suhl-ih-zuhm): relationship between two species in which one species benefits but the other is unaffected

elytra: wing cases that protect the hind wings

exoskeleton: the hard outer covering of an arthropod; contains chitin (KEYE-tuhn)

halteres (HOL-TIRS): a pair of clublike organs used by flies to balance in flight

hemolymph (HEE-muh-LIMPF): fluid pumped around the body of an arthropod by the heart; similar to vertebrate blood

hypermetamorphosis (HY-puh-MEH-tuh-MOR-fuh-suhs): type of insect development in which there is a radical change in form between successive larval stages

instars: stages of insect development separated by molts

invertebrate (IN-VUHR-tuh-bruht): animal without a backbone

larva (LAR-vuh): young form of insect that looks different from the adult, lives in a different habitat (type of place), and eats different foods

larviform: an adult insect that retains larval characters, such as a grublike body and small or absent legs

molt: shedding of the exoskeleton by an arthropod as it grows

mutualism (MYOO-chuh-wuh-LIH-zuhm): relationship between two different species in which both parties benefit

neurotoxin (NOOR-oh-TAHK-suhn): poison that acts on the nervous system

nymph (NIHMF): young form of insect that looks very similar to the adult and usually lives in a similar habitat (type of place)

ovipositor (OH-vuh-PAH-zuh-tuhr): tube on a female insect's abdomen for laying eggs

oxygen: gas in the air or dissolved in water that all organisms need to live

parasite: organism that feeds on another organism called a host; the host may be damaged but is not killed by the parasite

parthenogenesis (PAR-thuh-noh-JEH-nuh-suhs): production of young by female animals without fertilization by sperm from a male

pedipalps (PEH-duh-PALPS): pair of appendages near the mouthparts of spiders that are used for tasting and feeling; male spiders also use them to transfer sperm to females

pheromone (FEH-ruh-MOHN): chemical released by an insect, often to attract mates or to direct other insects to food

phoresy (fuh-REE-see): when a small animal hitches a ride on the body of a larger animal

placenta (pluh-SEN-tuh): organ that forms inside a female animal that nourishes the young before they are born

predator: an animal that feeds by catching and killing other animals

pronotum (PROH-noh-tuhm): shieldlike covering of the first segment of the thorax

pupa (PYOO-puh): stage during which a larva transforms into an adult insect

sperm: male sex cell that fuses with a female egg to create a new individual

symbiosis (SIM-bee-OH-suhs): a biological relationship between two different species

symmetry (SIM-uh-tree): when a shape looks the same on both sides

urticating (UHR-tuh-kay-ting) **hairs**: hairs on a spider's abdomen that irritate the eyes and nose of a predator; often released in a cloud

vertebrate (VUHR-tuh-bruht): animal with a backbone, such as a bird, reptile, or mammal

INDEX

Page numbers in **bold** refer to main articles; those in *italics* refer to picture captions.